Comments on other *Amazing Stories* from readers & reviewers

"Tightly written volumes filled with lots of wit and humour about famous and infamous Canadians."
Eric Shackleton, *The Globe and Mail*

"The heightened sense of drama and intrigue, combined with a good dose of human interest is what sets Amazing Stories *apart."*
Pamela Klaffke, *Calgary Herald*

"This is popular history as it should be... For this price, buy two and give one to a friend."
Terry Cook, a reader from Ottawa, on ***Rebel Women***

"Glasner creates the moment of the explosion itself in graphic detail...she builds detail upon gruesome detail to create a convincingly authentic picture."
Peggy McKinnon, *The Sunday Herald,* on ***The Halifax Explosion***

"It was wonderful...I found I could not put it down. I was sorry when it was completed."
Dorothy F. from Manitoba on ***Marie-Anne Lagimodière***

"Stories are rich in description, and bristle with a clever, stylish realness."
Mark Weber, *Central Alberta Advisor,* on ***Ghost Town Stories II***

"A compelling read. Bertin...has selected only the most intriguing tales, which she narrates with a wealth of detail."
Joyce Glasner, *New Brunswick Reader,* on ***Strange Events***

"The resulting book is one readers will want to share with all the women in their lives."
Lynn Martel, *Rocky Mountain Outlook,* on ***Women Explorers***

AMAZING STORIES

THE AVRO ARROW STORY

AMAZING STORIES

THE AVRO ARROW STORY

The Revolutionary Airplane and its Courageous Test Pilots

HISTORY

by Bill Zuk

PUBLISHED BY ALTITUDE PUBLISHING CANADA LTD.
1500 Railway Avenue, Canmore, Alberta T1W 1P6
www.altitudepublishing.com
1-800-957-6888

First published 2004

Publisher Stephen Hutchings
Associate Publisher Kara Turner
Series Editor Jill Foran
Editor Gayl Veinotte
Digital Photo Colouring Bryan Pezzi

We acknowledge the financial support of the Government of Canada through the Book Publishing Industry Development Program (BPIDP) for our publishing activities.

Altitude GreenTree Program
Altitude Publishing will plant twice as many trees as were used in the manufacturing of this product.

We acknowledge the support of the Canada Council for the Arts which in 2003 invested $21.7 million in writing and publishing throughout Canada.

Canada Council for the Arts Conseil des Arts du Canada

National Library of Canada Cataloguing in Publication Data

Zuk, Bill, 1947-
The Avro Arrow story / Bill Zuk.

(Amazing stories)
Includes bibliographical references.
ISBN 1-55153-978-0

1. Avro Arrow (Turbojet fighter plane) 2. A.V. Roe Canada--History. I. Title.
II. Series: Amazing stories (Canmore, Alta.)

TL685.3.Z83 2004 338.4'76237464'0971 C2004-904294-7

Printed and bound in Canada by Friesens
4 6 8 9 7 5

To all the Avroites, especially my dear friend,
Janusz Zurakowski.

Contents

Prologue

Streaking along the corridor from its home base of Malton, Ontario, to Lake Superior, the CF-105 Arrow, with a burst of its afterburners, accelerated effortlessly past the sound barrier, then zoomed straight up. Avro Aircraft Test Pilot Janusz "Zura" Zurakowski intended to fly RL-201, the first Mk.1 Arrow produced, faster and higher than ever before on this seventh test flight. The date was April 18, 1958.

The CF-105 clawed for altitude; Zura carefully set the dual throttles at just below maximum power as instructed by the Flight Engineering Department. After the first series of five test aircraft were evaluated, only then would the Arrow Mk.2 be used to set new world speed and altitude records.

Gerald Barbour had just finished his shift at the Avro plant, and, as was his habit, he parked his car alongside Dixon Road. A number of other cars eased to a stop behind him. Straining up into the sky, Barbour could make out the faint contrails of the Arrow and its chase planes.

High above, Zura stood the Arrow on its tail, pulling away from his chase planes as he passed 50,000 feet, still accelerating. Easing the throttles back, he noted while still climbing, the Machmeter had reached 1.52. Levelling out, he tested the handling characteristics of Canada's newest supersonic aircraft. Satisfied that the scheduled 40-minute flight was proceeding satisfactorily, he held station until the two chase planes finally came alongside.

Glancing over at test pilots Peter Cope in the CF-100 and Flight Lieutenant Jack Woodman in the Sabre, he gave them both a big grin. Although they were flying in the Royal Canadian Air Force's latest fighters, the CF-105 had left them far behind during this test fight. The incredible potential of the Avro Arrow was just beginning to be fulfilled.

Chapter 1
The Beginning of the End

As Lorne Ursel, one of Avro Canada's test pilots, overflew the Avro Aircraft plant in a thundering CF-100 Canuck prototype, he looked down at an incredible sight. The huge North and South parking lots were full. A few cars that had arrived late jockeyed for any spot still available. The enormous crowd of spectators, estimated at over 15,000, spilled from the parking lots and congregated at Hangar 1. This was an occasion that none of the employees from the Avro Aircraft and Avro Orenda Engine divisions at Malton, Ontario, wanted to miss. Sitting by itself in Hangar Bay 1 was the sole completed Avro Arrow. The date was October 4, 1957.

Ursel had been one of the RCAF acceptance pilots who had made a name for himself testing CF-100 fighters at the factory prior to their delivery to operational squadrons. He had left the military to work at Orenda Engines as an engineer, but when the opportunity arose to join Avro Aircraft, he became part of the Experimental Test Pilot group. Experimental flying on CF-100s at this stage had become quite mundane, but there were sometimes interesting aircraft to fly. On this day, Ursel had drawn the CF-100 "trial horse" as it was called in the Experimental Section. The prototype had been used to test the afterburning Orenda engine destined for the stillborn Mk.6 variant. The Mk.6 promised greater performance due to the newly developed "reheat" or afterburner that could provide greater thrust than the standard Orenda jet engine powering the earlier series of CF-100 fighters. This version was to have been the follow-up to the current series of production aircraft, the high-altitude Mk.5, but had been cancelled by the government in favour of the more advanced Avro Arrow.

The trial horse was a hybrid test "mule." With parts from different CF-100 Mk.4 and Mk.5 aircraft blended together, it had acquired the name "4 and one half." Extended tail pipes at the rear of the engines easily identified this prototype. The thrust in afterburning mode was impressive, producing a loud roar to announce its arrival. The Mk.6 trial horse was not a pilot favourite since the afterburners often did not light symmetrically, causing directional control problems. As Ursel formatted on the other aircraft overhead, he saw Avro Development test pilots Wladyslaw "Spud" Potocki,

Peter Cope, and Chief Production Test Pilot Chris Pike at the controls of production CF-100 Canucks Mk.3, 4, and 5. The four fighter aircraft would provide an aerial review of Avro products, "showing the flag" for the massive crowd gathering below and performing four high-speed flypasts just as the rollout occurred.

Near the ceremonial speakers' platform, at precisely 1400 hours, the RCAF band struck up *The Knightsbridge March,* serenading the crowd of onlookers who had filled the seats set up in front of Hangar Bay 1. Avro office employees passed out copies of the official program that listed the events of the day, indicating that there would be more than two-dozen dignitaries in attendance. The "suits" were already seated at the speakers' platform and included representatives from the parent company, A.V. Roe Canada, the Canadian government, and notables from the ranks of Canada's military and aviation industry. As befitted the occasion and their role as partners in defence of North America, members of the U.S. Air Force (USAF) were also in attendance.

Since 1959 would mark the nation's 50th anniversary of powered flight, Canadian aviation luminary John A.D. McCurdy, the first to fly in Canada, was the special guest of honour. The post office had recently announced a commemorative stamp to mark the anniversary. It featured McCurdy's "Silver Dart" flanked by a trio of silvery darts in the sky that were clearly Avro Arrows.

Frederick T. Smye, vice president of Avro Aircraft

Limited, rose to begin the formal part of the afternoon. "This ceremony today is one of great significance to all of us at Avro and, we would like to think, to the Canadian aviation industry. The Arrow ... demonstrates the capability of Canadian technology, and represents a substantial Canadian contribution to the western world."

Air Marshal and Chief of Air Staff Hugh L. Campbell was next on the roster. He elaborated succinctly the role that the Avro Arrow would play in North America's air defence system. "The planned performance of this aircraft is such that it can effectively meet and deal with any likely bomber threat to this continent over the next decade. We in the air force look upon this aircraft as one component of a complex and elaborate air defence system covering, in the first instance, the whole of the North American continent, extending from Labrador to Hudson Bay to the Queen Charlotte Islands."

Defence Minister George Pearkes, who would become instrumental in the fate of the Arrow, reached up, and with a flourish, tugged on a golden lanyard as a signal to open the hangar doors. As one, the crowd surged forward to catch a glimpse into the dark bay at the majestic white bird, perched on its thin, spindly legs. At least that is the recollection of a young George Foley, who had accompanied his family on this wondrous day. His father was a tool-and-die operator at Avro.

A small tow truck eased the Arrow out into the bright daylight. The crowd cheered and clapped. Photographers and

The Avro Arrow rollout brought over 13,000 guests to the plant.

reporters scurried about the edges of the throng. Company executives mingled with shop-floor workers, as they all pressed closer to the aircraft. Nearly unnoticed, Avro's chief development test pilot, Jan Zurakowski, circled the Arrow slowly, gazing up at the complex undercarriage.

Despite what the company president, Crawford Gordon Jr., had announced to the assembled media, the Arrow was not ready for its flight test. As it sat, the aircraft had no radar, avionics (electronics used to pilot the aircraft), or weapons.

The first aircraft off the assembly line was slated for a rigorous series of proving flights, which required the installation of an extensive array of instrumentation packed into its weapons bay. After refitting, engineers devised a prolonged schedule for ground testing of all systems that would extend far into the next year. The rollout was a public relations exercise.

Late in the afternoon, six-year-old George Foley lingered at a roped-off stanchion when a newspaper photographer spotted the diminutive figure next to the Avro Arrow. Appearing the next day in countless publications, the photograph dramatically framed the "future looking at the future."

At the precise moment the rollout ceremony ended, high in the heavens, a silvery globe blinked a steady mechanical signature to its launch headquarters in the nether regions of Soviet Central Asia. Sputnik had just completed its first orbit of Earth.

In Malton, the first news of the Sputnik satellite crackled over Avro engineer Robert Lindley's car radio. After the ceremony, Lindley had been delegated to escort the American guests to the airport. The stunned entourage listened as the radio broadcast outlined the historic flight of the Sputnik. Lindley thought to himself, "That's it, they destroyed our rollout!"

The next morning, newspaper headlines all over the world carried the Sputnik story as their banner, and, even in Toronto, the rollout of the Arrow was relegated to secondary status. Scientific, government, and military circles recorded a watershed date, but the true portent of the Sputnik and the rocket that guided it into orbit was still to come.

Chapter 2
In the Footfalls of Titans

Avro Canada's origins can be traced back to a time when the world had been at war for over three years. Across Europe and Asia, the Axis powers had established vast empires. Only Great Britain and her sprawling Commonwealth, the besieged Soviet Union, and lately the United States, which had been forced into the conflict, stood in the way of annihilation by Hitler, Mussolini, and Tojo.

In Canada, a mobilization for war that had begun in 1939 was now seeing progress. Prime Minister Mackenzie King's wartime Cabinet had been similarly mobilized, its most crucial departments led by a select group of powerful men. The leading figure in Cabinet was C.D. Howe, who oversaw the Ministry of Transportation and the Ministry of

Munitions and Supply. His presence would dominate the effort to win the war on Canada's home front.

Clarence Decataur Howe's background was remarkable. By his own words, he was a "Canadian by choice." Born in 1886 in Waltham, Massachusetts, Howe had family connections on both sides of the border. C.D. was related to Joseph Howe, the one-time premier of Nova Scotia and member of John A. Macdonald's cabinet. Following graduation from the Massachusetts Institute of Technology with a degree in science, Howe moved to Canada in 1908 to become the first professor of civil engineering at Dalhousie University in Halifax.

After five years at Dalhousie, Howe was lured to the west to build the necessary infrastructure of grain elevators and transport hubs for a surging grain economy. He recognized that the small hamlet of Port Arthur on the shores of Lake Superior was an ideal terminus, and on his own initiative, developed a marshy stretch of lakefront and set the stage for the future grain port. Resigning his government post, Howe established an engineering consulting firm that built the Port Arthur pier and foundations, despite the brutal weather of the winter of 1917.

Howe and Company then turned to construction projects including docks, bridges, and factories. Specializing in the construction of towering grain elevators, the company prospered until the Great Depression. Howe's partners eventually left and Howe turned to politics.

Not a polished orator by any means, Howe was, nevertheless,

a brawler. Although independently wealthy from his many years in the business world, he had the appearance of an everyman. His combative nature, combined with an arduous campaign of whistle-stopping and constant handshaking, proved to be decisive in the first of many elections he would win. Liberal leader Mackenzie King was similarly swept into power with a massive majority, and chose Howe for the newly created post of Minister of Transport. Howe immediately began to cut a swath through bureaucracy, seeing himself much more as an implementer than a policymaker. His no-nonsense approach, which some felt was bellicose, belied a careful study of the issues.

Canada's first Minister of Transport was particularly interested in establishing a strong Canadian presence in the growing field of civil aviation. Unemployed workers of the "Dirty '30s" built airstrips across the country, and Trans-Canada Airlines (Air Canada's predecessor) was established as a Crown corporation. Howe helped to establish the National Harbours Board and centralize the administration of ports. He reformed the debt-laden CNR and created the Canadian Broadcasting Corporation. In all his departments, his motto was to increase efficiency and accountability. That emphasis would prove to be vitally important during the war years.

All these measures helped to pull the country's transportation network out of the Depression, preparing it for the incredible challenge that it would soon face. Canada's war effort of 1939–1945 necessitated a dollar expenditure that was ten times greater than that of the Great War of 1914–1918. The means to deliver the weapons of war fell to the new Department of Munitions and Supply and to C.D. Howe. Within months, he created a multitude of Crown corporations and boards that would serve to provide the necessary raw materials, establish manufacturing facilities, and create supply lines to meet the military requirements of Great Britain, the United States, and Canada. Howe's enthusiasm and drive seemed to transfer into energizing the war effort of the ordinary citizen.

Howe knew that what Canada lacked was not money or resources but "managerial skill." From all over Canada, he recruited his "boys." The press called them the "buck-a-year men," but they were the best in the business and now the business was winning a war.

Industrial wartime expansion reached across the nation. Shipbuilding on both coasts contributed over 400 vessels, ranging from more than 100 plodding but useful for Corvettes North Atlantic convoy duty to innumerable merchant ships. Arms and munitions factories were converted from peacetime automobile and locomotive production. Industrialist James. E. Hahn rebuilt the John Inglis Company at Long Branch, a Toronto suburb. The facility employed 17,000 workers during the war and turned out more machine guns than any other individual firm in the British Empire. Final totals of Bren guns, Browning aircraft machine guns, .55-calibre Boys anti-tank rifles and 9-mm pistols reached

The Avro Aircraft plant at shift change c. 1949.

some half-million weapons. Hahn's business acumen was also called upon in other war production, specifically aircraft manufacture.

National Steel Car Corporation, headquartered in Hamilton and predominately a manufacturer of railway rolling stock, had begun to produce munitions prior to 1939. They established a massive manufacturing facility in Malton to undertake the construction of the Westland Lysander Army co-operation aircraft and later, the Avro Anson light bomber/trainer for both the RCAF and Great Britain's Royal

Air Force (RAF). The Malton plant would become the largest of Canada's pre-war aircraft factories.

In 1941, Great Britain's A.V. Roe (Avro) and Company Ltd. turned to Canada to build Lancaster bombers. The British Supply Council had attempted to ensure continuous supply of the much-needed heavy bomber by "farming out" production to North America. When U.S. factories were unable to accept new production orders, the task was redirected to Canada.

At a meeting in the Washington, D.C. headquarters of the British Supply Council, C.D. Howe led a delegation of Canadian industrialists and military representatives, including his erstwhile right-hand man, the redoubtable E.P. Taylor, who served as the chairman of the meeting. Taylor, who was later to gain fame in the horseracing world as the owner of the legendary "Northern Dancer," was already acknowledged as a great horse-trader in the business arena. At the back of the room, one of the junior members of the committee, Mr. Frederick Smye from Fairchild Aircraft, took copious notes. Taylor began the meeting by relating news from his recent visit to England, where the expatriate Canadian, Lord Beaverbrook, the Minister of Aircraft Production, had pleaded for Canada to produce the RAF's newest heavy bomber, the "Lanc." Howe and Taylor laid out the provisions for Canadian production to begin. National Steel Car in Malton, which had, until recently, been tooling up for production of the American B-26 Marauder medium bomber, received the Lancaster contract.

Manufacturing the Avro Lancaster would be a daunting challenge, but the rewards would be great for Canada. As the most venerated British bomber of the Second World War, the Lancaster, flown by RAF, RCAF, and Commonwealth crews, saw most of its service in massive night raids on occupied Europe and Germany. Equipped with four Rolls-Royce Merlin engines and a sturdy airframe, the Lancaster was able to carry varying loads of bombs and incendiaries, including the devastating 22,000-lb "Grand Slam," the heaviest bomb carried by any aircraft during the Second World War. In the famed 1943 "Dam Busters" raid, specially modified Lancasters dropped bouncing bombs on the dams of Germany's industrial Ruhr Valley from an altitude of only 60 feet above water. The sustained night bombing campaign by the RAF eventually led to the destruction of the Nazi war machine. The Avro Lancaster's legendary status derived from its ability to withstand enormous damage, yet still return its crews safely home.

The Lancaster and its birth can be attributed mainly to one man at A.V. Roe — its colourful managing director, Roy "Dobbie" Dobson. Even though the design team, led by Chief Designer Roy Chadwick, created the technical drawings and was responsible for the Avro (type 679) Manchester, from which the Lancaster sprung, it was Dobson who fought and won a battle against the British Air Ministry to launch the new bomber.

The twin-engined Manchester had flown in 1939 and

entered service, despite persistent and harrowing problems with its new Rolls-Royce Vulture I engines. The Vulture was an unproven design that had a protracted and troubled development. Recurrent engine failures and the subsequent loss of aircraft marked its short operational life. In 1940, A.V. Roe was assigned the ignominious duty of scrapping the Manchester and working as a sub-contractor for its rival, the Handley-Page Halifax bomber.

Dobbie reacted to the news that Avro would be building its competitor's aircraft as a supreme insult. "Didn't those at the top know whom they were dealing with? I know we've had nothing but trouble with that damn thing, but we can fix it. Even if I have to go to Beaverbrook myself, I'll reverse this bloody decision!"

When informed of the cancellation of the Manchester bomber, Chadwick and a small engineering team, including junior member, James C. Floyd, redesigned the Manchester into a 4-engined bomber using proven Rolls-Royce Merlin engines. The design of the proposed Manchester III merged the fuselage and an enlarged version of its wing to the Merlin power plants. When members of the Ministry of Aircraft Production arrived at A.V. Roe in July 1940, Dobson vigorously campaigned for a chance to build this new design. He then complained directly to Lord Beaverbrook, the head of the ministry, but was told that no Merlin engines were to be released for experimentation. When Dobson persisted, Beaverbrook retorted, "You can just dig for them!"

Dobson did just that. Appealing to Lord Hives, the director of Rolls Royce, he heard the same answer that Beaverbrook had given him — Merlins were needed for the Spitfire and Hurricane fighters that defended Britain. In spite of his reputation as a rough character, Dobson could also display an amazing dexterity and charm. He convinced Hives to "loan" him just four Merlins, swiped right off two prototype Beaufighter fighters. When he rang back to Chadwick with the go-ahead, he was asked if Beaverbrook had changed his mind.

"No," Dobson roared. "We're going ahead with it, boy."

Now called the Lancaster, the prototype flew for the first time on January 9, 1941. When a dumbfounded Beaverbrook learned of the successful trials of a new Avro bomber with Merlin engines, Dobson curtly informed him "that he had dug for them." The British Air Ministry accepted the Lancaster immediately. A report deploring the methods used to obtain the contract circulated through the department. Dobson merely chortled.

When production of the Avro Lancaster came to Canada, the fate of the project became tied to two visionaries — Dobbie from England and C.D. from Canada. In order to build the Avro Lancaster, C.D. Howe would have to deal with National Steel Car's problems. Since the sudden death of its dynamic president, Robert J. Magor, early in 1942, the company seemed to be floundering. Howe was known for taking to task any wartime enterprise that he felt wasn't performing efficiently or, worst of all, "profited" from the war. He had earlier forced a West Coast ship manufacturer to remit over $2 million in profit.

What Howe now saw in Malton was an extravagant and inefficient organization fraught with internal bickering centred on the new administration of R.S. Hart. The new president had antagonized senior management at Malton with his resistance to diversifying into aircraft manufacture. Aircraft contracts stalled and a number of executives resigned in protest. The discontent in the executive suite, however, was nothing compared to the anger on the shop floor. Dave Boyd, the general manager at the Malton operation and a roll-up-his-sleeves kind of guy, finally decided he couldn't take it any longer.

Rumours about Malton's troubles reached C.D. Howe, himself. Upon receiving a telegram from Boyd that outlined the issues at the plant and indicated that the imminent Lancaster production contract was threatened, Howe forcefully took matters into his own hands. He immediately directed all 35 employees that had signed the telegram to report to the boardroom to meet his representative.

On November 5, 1942, J.P. Bickell, one of Howe's buck-a-year men and a well-known pre-war industrialist, burst into the office. The assembled employee group expected to be fired on the spot. Bickell surveyed the scene.

"As of this moment," he said, "this company has been expropriated by His Majesty's Government, and I am now the Chairman of the Board." Indicating to Boyd, he continued, "and this is your general manager." With that declaration, National Steel Car Corporation became Victory Aircraft Limited, another of the burgeoning group of Crown corporations Howe administered.

Victory Aircraft immediately began hiring more staff and assembling a production team. James Hahn was brought in to be a director and vice president. Efficiently organizing the production lines, he had the plant turning out airframes and receiving Packard-Merlin power plants from the Packard Company in the United States. The Canadian-built Lancaster X differed subtly from its British antecedent in that it used a combination of British and American equipment. After the first British "pattern aircraft" arrived, KB700 (later code named LQ-Q and bearing the appropriate nomenclature "Queenie") became the first production Lanc, flying on August 1, 1943.

Boyd's workforce stepped up production to one Lancaster a day until the end of the war. Small improvements to equipment and high standards in assembly made the Lancaster X, in some ways, superior to the British-built Lancaster. Only one was lost in the trans-Atlantic shipments to operational units. Dobson's man at the plant, Alf Stewart, began to send back glowing reports on the Canadian operation.

Intrigued by these reports, Dobson, accompanied by Sir Frank Spriggs, the managing director of Hawker-Siddeley Group, the controlling interest behind A.V. Roe, flew across the Atlantic in September 1943 for the first of two supervisory visits. At a time when any ocean crossing was perilous, Dobson was adamant that he had to see the Malton factory for himself.

The danger in the North Atlantic was real. On December 14, 1940, on one of his voyages to England, a U-boat had torpedoed C.D. Howe's ship. Characteristically, Howe had taken charge of the lifeboat and 34 sailors and passengers. Miraculously, the survivors were rescued by the captain of a tramp steamer who had disobeyed orders to come back to the sinking ship. On that trip, Howe had been briefed on future British aircraft projects, including the Avro Lancaster.

Dobson had intended to be present at the rollout and maiden flight of the first Canadian-built Lancaster. Victory Aircraft didn't wait for him; by the time Dobbie arrived, KB700 was already engaged in test flights. Dobson was amazed at what was going on at Victory. The plant hummed with approximately 8000 men and women steadily at work on three eight-hour shifts. Workers bustled with pride at their achievements and a general spirit of camaraderie prevailed. Pay was modest, but at $1 an hour, it allowed most the luxury of a home and car. Nearby Malton village was populated predominantly by Victory employees. Dobson followed up an extensive round of meetings with aviation and government officials by interviewing C.D. Howe himself. A magnificent new prospect was beginning to form in his mind.

Victory Aircraft-built Avro Lancaster (with later RCAF markings).

High over the skies of Nazi-occupied France, KB726, a newly built Lancaster Mk.X from Canada was on its fourth mission. Code-marked "VR-A," the Lancaster had recently been assigned to 419 Squadron of the No. 6 RCAF Bomber Group. Except for the flight engineer, F/O (Flight Officer) Roy Vigars, it was an all-Canadian crew under the command of F/O Arthur de Breyne. The previous night, the bomber had blown up the bridge and crossroads at Constances, but on this night, June 12, 1944, the ominous 13th mission for the crew, everything went wrong. Coned by searchlights over Cambrai, pilot de Breyne corkscrewed the Lancaster away from the anti-aircraft guns and down to an altitude of 2000 feet. Tail-gunner F/O Pat Brophy spotted a Junkers Ju-88 night-fighter closing in and shouted out a warning over the intercom. Slipping under the twisting bomber, the Ju-88 fired, hitting the Lancaster twice in the port wing, knocking out both engines and setting the fuel in the wing tanks on fire. A third cannon shell struck the fuselage between the mid-upper gunner's station manned by W/O (Warrant Officer) Andrew Mynarsky, and the rear turret, starting a hydraulic oil fire.

The blazes that engulfed the mortally wounded bomber left no choices for the crew. While de Bryne wrestled with the controls, crewmen at the forward stations abandoned the aircraft. Mynarsky heard the bailout command, but immediately turned back to check on Brophy. He could just make out the tail gunner struggling with the turret's jammed escape door. Despite the flames around him, Mynarsky tried to help his trapped tail-gunner. Scant moments later, the fire reached his clothing and parachute. Brophy tried to wave him away, but Mynarsky heroically continued to hack away at the turret with a fire axe, and even tried to pry it free with his bare hands.

Finally, Mynarsky was forced to quit his efforts. Although he was ablaze from waist to foot, he stood at the escape hatch and saluted his friend before jumping out of the bomber to his death. The only person left aboard was the tail-gunner when the Lancaster crashed heavily into a farmyard. The bomber careened into a tree, ripping the intact turret section away from the rear fuselage. The impact snapped the turret doors open, allowing a dazed Brophy to crawl away from the exploding wreckage. Brophy's miraculous survival eventually led to Andrew Mynarsky's posthumous award of the Victoria Cross, the last such medal presented in the Second World War.

Andrew Mynarsky's heroism was only one of many sagas of the Avro Lancaster. Some 7400 Lancasters were manufactured between 1940 and 1946, with production in both Great Britain and Canada. Eventually over 9500 employees were hired for the Lancaster production line at Victory Aircraft Limited. By war's end, Victory had built 3634 Avro aircraft: 3197 Ansons, 430 Lancasters, 6 Lincoln bombers, and a single York airliner.

Chapter 3
Building the Team

The last of the 430 Avro Lancaster X bombers, FM229, rolled out of its assembly bay at Victory Aircraft in September 1945. The crews that stayed for the celebration knew it was more than the end of the production run — Victory was finished. With only 300 of the workforce remaining and no new contracts, the prospects for the company were dim. The recently knighted Sir Roy Dobson tried to sell the Canadian military and airlines the new Lincoln bomber and York transports, both developments of the Lancaster. Although pattern aircraft were constructed at Victory Aircraft, neither project progressed past that point.

VJ Day signalled the victory over Japan and the end of hostilities, but at Malton, layoff notices were being prepared for all employees including Dave Boyd, the leader of the "shop-floor revolt." He left the aviation industry for good. In the backrooms, Sir Roy worked feverishly to save the company. He sought out C.D. Howe, now the Minister of Reconstruction, a new department responsible for Canada's post-war economy. Dobson offered to purchase Victory and its massive factory. Howe was astounded by the offer as it came at exactly the juncture when a decision had to be made regarding the future of the plant. To the members of the Hawker Siddeley Group, facing similar problems with a surplus of factories and equipment in England, the deal was known as "Dobson's Folly." Even Howe remarked, "Dobson had more guts than brains."

Howe hammered out an agreement with Dobson that created a new company with a decidedly Canadian mandate. The requirement to carry out research and development in aviation in Canada led to Dobson also acquiring Turbo Research Limited, where the "Chinook," Canada's first jet engine, was designed and tested. The Nobel Test Establishment at Parry Sound was another facility thrown into the deal. A.V. Roe Canada Limited, more commonly known as Avro Canada, born on November 2, 1945 from the former Crown corporations, had only one employee — Frederick Timothy Smye. Until the end of his career, Smye proudly wore Avro Employee Badge No. 1.

A.V. Roe Canada transferred staff and equipment from the former jet engine group to the new Gas Turbine Division, across the street from the aircraft factory. With the capability to design and manufacture aircraft and engines, Dobson and a small skeleton staff laid out an ambitious agenda for the future: the design and construction of a new, advanced, jet engine; the first jet fighter for the RCAF; and, most audaciously, the first jet-powered airliner in the world!

Hiring 300 former Victory Aircraft employees allowed the aircraft factory to come back to life. Smye, formerly with Howe's Department of Munitions and Supply and lately with Federal Aircraft in Montreal, became the general manager. He made sure that the best possible workforce was assembled. The first contracts had nothing to do with aviation. The giant manufacturing plant shook off the cobwebs with the mundane tasks of turning out plastic hairbrushes, truck fenders, and Cockshutt tractor parts. Their initial aircraft contracts involved repair and overhaul work with Hawker Sea Fury fighters and B-25 Mitchell bombers.

Then came the first major contracts to convert the remaining fleet of Lancaster bombers. The RCAF's post-war need for coastal patrol, air search-and-rescue, and photo-reconnaissance led to the decision to pull the venerable Lancaster aircraft out of storage. The return of the heavy bombers to the factory for conversion allowed A.V. Roe to expand their operation. Dobson assembled a very talented design team: key Canadian personnel, such as Stan Cyma, Jack Millie, Mario Pesando, and Bryan Wood from Victory; James A. Chamberlin from Noorduyn Aircraft; English engineers Edgar H. Atkin, Robert N. "Bob" Lindley, and James C. "Jim" Floyd from A.V. Roe Limited (Manchester); John C.M. Frost from de Havilland (U.K.); and finally, Polish expatriate Waclaw Czerwinski.

Their first A.V. Roe Canada project was designed with one customer in mind: TCA, (Trans-Canada Airlines, now Air Canada), C.D. Howe's "baby." Jim Floyd had drawn up blueprints for a "30-seater Transport Aircraft" while still in England and now he and his design were transferred to Canada. TCA President H.J. Symington signed a letter of intent with A.V. Roe Canada that carefully framed the conditions for a further contract. The original design was based on two Rolls-Royce AJ65 axial-flow engines, but problems with the project began at this point when Rolls-Royce refused to provide the engines.

The airliner was hastily redesigned into a four-engined version, powered by the proven RR Derwent centrifugal flow engine. Named the C102 "Jetliner," work proceeded to the production drawing stage, but TCA was clearing showing signs of "cold feet." Being the principal sponsor of the first jet airliner would have put Trans-Canada Airlines in the forefront of the world's airlines, but it would also mean operating under intense scrutiny. Symington made the extraordinary decision to approach C.D. Howe, Minister of Reconstruction, to be released from their letter of intent, citing a host of technical issues arising from the redesign. The main concern was operating costs for a radically new type of airliner. By 1947, both Howe and Dobson were at a crossroads with A.V. Roe Canada, facing either triumph or disaster.

With over 200 engineers and technical staff employed in the Design Office, and two other groundbreaking projects also underway, all of the research and development work would be in jeopardy unless Howe came to the rescue. Realizing the fate of the company hung in the balance, Howe provided $1.5 million in development funds, enough to keep A.V. Roe Canada in business. On the drawing board was Chief Engineer Edgar Atkin and Project Engineer John C.M. Frost's XC-100 fighter. It was Avro Canada's submission to meet the RCAF's "Air-7-Issue 2" specifications for a Canadian-designed fighter to protect Canada's arctic frontier. More importantly, the XC-100 had a new jet engine, the TR-5 Orenda 1 jet engine, based on the earlier Chinook design. The Orenda was destined to power all of Avro's future aircraft and become a commercial success when it was sold to other manufacturers. Today, Orenda jet engine technology remains the sole legacy of this company.

Even without TCA's backing, Dobson gave Jim Floyd and his team the go-ahead to complete the first jetliner. By the time CF-EJD-X, the Avro C102 prototype, began preparation for its flight test, the company realized it was in a race to get the first jet-powered airliner into the air. Across the Atlantic, de Havilland Aircraft was putting the finishing touches to the DH. 106 Comet at their factory in Hatfield, England.

Both Geoffrey de Havilland and Sir Roy Dobson had

staked their reputations and their company's fortunes on their jet airliner projects. The Avro C102 Jetliner had a lot in common with the Comet. Each design had its origins in the wartime British civil air transport planning committee. Research into jet-engine technology had formed the basis of preliminary proposals by both companies. Even though the Comet was designed for transatlantic service, the designs called for a similar passenger capacity and would operate at about the same speed and altitude.

During the spring and summer of 1949, both the Comet and Jetliner entered the final stages of taxi testing. Through an unfortunate combination of events, the Avro Jetliner lost the competition to be first into the air. Runway resurfacing of the Malton airport along with last-minute repairs to the engine nacelles delayed the Jetliner's maiden flight. When test pilot James "Jimmy" Orrell, on loan from Avro (U.K.), flew the C102 on August 10, 1949, the Comet had already been flying for 13 days and had been heralded as the world's first jet airliner. Coming in second was small consolation for Floyd and Dobson.

But there was a brief moment of acclaim for the fledgling company. Shortly after the completion of the first test flights, the Jetliner garnered headlines all over the world...

Jim Floyd stared out into the morning mist over Manhattan's skyline. He motioned to Fred Smye sitting across from him to look out his window. The Jetliner flight from Toronto to New

The majestic Avro Jetliner in flight.

York had taken less than an hour. Pilot Don Rogers would log the flying time as 59 minutes and 56 seconds at an impressive average speed of 400 mph. It was April 18, 1950.

Rogers entered the landing circuit for Idlewild Airport (today, Kennedy International) slipping in behind a Convair 240. Even though the piston-engined transport was one of the newest in the sky, compared to the Avro C102 Jetliner, it looked positively antiquated. The Jetliner could operate routinely at 30,000 feet and cruised at twice the speed of the latest piston airliners. The tower picked up the sleek silver and yellow jet aircraft as it turned downwind over the outskirts of the majestic city. Mike Cooper-Slipper in the right-hand seat had just relayed the message to Rogers that they had clearance to land.

Even though Avro had cleared official hurdles in applying for permission for the flight, a last minute hitch cropped up. The novelty of a jet airliner had taken U.S. airport officials by surprise. The airport manager of the nearby LaGuardia Airfield insisted that the "fire-spitting" jet airliner shouldn't be allowed anywhere near LaGuardia. An Avro representative on the ground finally convinced him that there was no danger of fire.

Onboard the Jetliner, the subject of fire was also a concern, but in a different way. Flight Engineer Bill Baker smiled broadly as he produced the glowing peace pipe Toronto Mayor Hiram McCallum had sent along with a massive scroll bearing greetings from the Canadian International Trade Fair. The pipe had gone out in mid-flight, but Baker had furtively relit it and returned it to the flight deck.

Rogers made one ceremonial pass over the field and then swept in to make a graceful landing. Reporters and photographers, scrambling for ideal vantage points, quickly joined a large assemblage of airport and government officials. The crew shut down and then appeared at the cockpit door, resplendent in bright white coveralls. Rogers was carrying a Native headdress and held the smoking peace pipe to be presented to a representative of the mayor of New York. As the crew descended to bursting flashbulbs, the Jetliner passengers joined them. Floyd and Smye were accompanied by Mario Pesando from Avro's engineering department. The Jetliner had set a number of records with this flight. It was the first international jet airliner flight and the first time airmail had been delivered by jet. The Toronto postmaster had placed aboard a small sack of mail. More importantly, the Jetliner had proven to be a revelation to the United States; no American competitor even existed on drawing boards. It would be seven years before the world-class Boeing 707 would begin its route trials. Over 500 newspapers and periodicals countrywide, as well as local radio stations, covered the story of the Jetliner's visit. Most telling was the *Air Trails* magazine headline: "What Happened to the Great American Aircraft Industry?" The New York trip was a triumphal visit for Avro Canada; unfortunately, it would not lead to any sales.

Back at Malton, the XC-100, now re-christened the CF-100, was nearing the date of its first flight. But behind the scenes, John Frost was desperately trying to rectify a potentially deadly flaw. Without Frost's knowledge, Chief Aerodynamicist Jim Chamberlin had moved the two jet engines back through the centre section of the aircraft to cure a weight distribution problem, but had notched the wing spar to accommodate the relocation of the engines. The weakened spar was a "soft spot" that allowed the wings to flex dangerously. Even after the arrival of the flamboyant Gloster Aircraft Company test pilot, Squadron Leader Bill Waterton, also on loan to the company, the CF-100 prototype #18101 was not really ready for its flight tests. Waterton flew the first CF-100 Mk.1, coded FB-D on January 19, 1950, the weakened spar problem still in place.

His subsequent test flights showed just how dangerous the spar was. Over Toronto during a demonstration at the Canadian National Exhibition, Waterton reported that he heard a crack "like a thunderbolt." He gingerly landed the aircraft, but further flights would be on hold until the spar could be repaired. In an engineering "blitz," Waclaw Czerwinski, leader of the Stress Office, designed a strengthened pin-joint that was retrofitted to all prototype and production CF-100s.

In the same year, the Orenda jet engine successfully completed its in-flight testing in a modified Lancaster that carried two Orenda turbojets, in pods, in place of the outboard Merlin engines. The Orenda later powered all production CF-100s as well as the Canadair Sabre series of fighters. The team of Avro pilots Don Rogers and Mike Cooper-Slipper, along with flight engineer Bill Baker, began setting a string of local, national, and international records with the Jetliner throughout North America. Other than minor setbacks, the Jetliner appeared to be a success story. Floyd commented, "The flight program went unbelievably well. Airline flight times were halved by the Jetliner on inter-city flights all over the U.S. and Canada; many U.S. airline executives were carried on these flights and, without exception, were enthusiastic about the aircraft."

All three A.V. Roe Canada projects were "off the ground" when Cold War tensions exploded into a real war in Korea. In response to a Canadian commitment to the conflict, C.D. Howe instructed Avro to "ramp up" the production of the CF-100 fighter and, without notice, ordered an end to the Jetliner. The Canadian government's decision came down just as contract negotiations were underway with National Airlines, Trans World Airlines, and the USAF. Even Howard Hughes, the eccentric millionaire, had expressed interest in the Jetliner, but C.D. Howe was adamant. The CF-100 fighter program had to have priority. Floyd had tears in his eyes as he watched the second Jetliner prototype being broken up at the back of the factory.

C.D. Howe had been observing the unsteady progress of Avro with alarm. When the RCAF informed him that the CF-100's operational deployment was being delayed due to problems with the design, he blew up at Dobson. "Fix the problems with the CF-100 and with the damn company and do it now!"

Sir Roy Dobson, never one to be called a diplomat, knew what he had to do and knew just the man to do it. Crawford Gordon Jr. was a star in industry and finance in Canada. President of Canadian General Electric at the age of 28, he was another of Howe's buck-a-year men and the "Boy Wonder" of the Ministry of Munitions and Supply in wartime.

When Dobson plucked Gordon from his job as CEO of the English Electric Company in Canada, Howe was furious at the loss of a key player in the Canadian post-war recovery. Yet, he knew that Gordon was the man who could straighten Avro out.

Crawford Gordon Jr. arrived at A.V. Roe Canada like a whirlwind in 1951. By the end of the year, he had restructured the company and made sure the planes were there when the military needed them. Recognizing Jim Floyd and Fred Smye as major talents, he gave Floyd control of the CF-100 program, removed Atkin as chief designer, moved Frost to the Special Projects Group, and divided the operation into the Aircraft Division, with Smye as general manager, putting the Gas Turbine Division under Tom McCrae. Avro moved into series production of the CF-100 fighter and simultaneously began planning for its eventual replacement.

Chapter 4
Test Flying at Avro Canada

In the war-torn skies above Europe and Asia, a number of young men had made the difference between victory and defeat. Most had piloted the lethal fighter planes that were the defenders of Poland, France, England, Singapore, and Ceylon. As they learned their deadly craft, some of the men began to consider a life in aviation after the war.

The stories of A.V. Roe Canada's test pilots are intertwined with the amazing aircraft they flew. Yet each of the test pilots who worked at Avro had already lived an extraordinary life before joining the Avro team.

Chief Test Pilot Don Rogers headed the Flight Operations Department, directing all the flights of the C102 Jetliner, CF-100 Canuck, and CF-105 Arrow test programs. He had deep roots in the company, first as a test pilot with National Steel, and then continuing during World War Two with Victory Aircraft as the chief development pilot of the Avro Lancaster series. Racking up thousands of hours in both testing and ferrying missions, he gained a reputation not only as a precise and smooth flier, but also as a skilled manager. Rogers was the command pilot of all the unusual Lancaster variants, including the wild and woolly Orenda engine test-bed. The two jet engines on the ends of the wings replacing the usual Merlin piston engines were powerful enough to make this hybrid the fastest Lancaster ever.

Although Rogers would never admit to it, the Orenda test-bed was used to "spook" the Americans on alert across the border at Niagara Falls. Staging over Lake Ontario well below radar, the Lancaster would pop up and instantly appear on the USAF radar scopes. The sudden appearance of an intruder would cause all sorts of panic on the U.S. side. When tired, old Air National Guard P-47 Thunderbolts would be scrambled, the Orenda Lancaster would fire up the jets and effortlessly "squirt away." The USAF was not amused by the Avro stunts.

Another favourite trick of the pilots flying this test-bed was shutting down the Merlin engines and sweeping over an airfield with just the jet engines going. The nearly silent test aircraft would swoop over and twirl away to the astonishment of spectators on the ground.

Thomas Paul "Mike" Cooper-Slipper, Rogers' second-in-command, carried out all the Jetliner demonstration flights both in Canada and the United States with Rogers. Howard Hughes, an eminent pilot who had set countless world records between his bouts of paranoia, was a particular fan of Rogers. Rogers also assumed the mantle as the primary pilot in the CF-100 program.

Mike Cooper-Slipper, DFC, was famous for ramming a Dornier bomber with his Hawker Hurricane fighter during the Battle of Britain. He somehow survived and went on to down a total of nine aircraft that fiery summer. In 1941, he flew out one of the last Hurricanes as the Japanese overran Singapore. Running out of fuel over the jungles of Burma, Cooper-Slipper was forced to bail out and endure a gruelling week-long trek back to safety.

After flying as a test pilot in England, Mike Cooper-Slipper came to Canada in 1947 to join Avro as an engine fitter assigned to the Chinook engine project. He was soon transferred to flight testing as the first post-war test pilot employed at A.V. Roe Canada. Cooper-Slipper began flying overhauled B-25 Mitchell and Lancaster aircraft, before being assigned to the Jetliner and CF-100 programs. Later, as the chief test pilot at Avro's sister operation, Orenda Engines, Cooper-Slipper carried out the development testing of the Orenda engine.

As the pilot of the Orenda Lancaster during an air demonstration over Malton, Mike Cooper-Slipper inadvertently became the pilot of the first Avro "glider." Buzzing the field in

Avro CF-100 Canuck fighters on patrol.

the usual fashion, flying only on jets, he shouted out to start the Merlins. His engineer promptly shut down the jet engines. Down on the deck with no altitude to spare, Cooper-Slipper somehow managed to relight the jets, but not before he gave the spectators a close-up of a completely silent Lancaster bomber flying like the proverbial brick.

Cooper-Slipper flew all the CF-100 versions as well as the superb Orenda-powered Canadair Sabre. For a time, the RCAF Sabre squadrons had the bragging rights to flying the world's best fighter. When the CF-105 Arrow entered flight-test, Mike Cooper-Slipper was assigned to the converted Boeing B-47 bomber that served as the Orenda Iroquois test bed.

During the early period of test flying at Avro Canada, a pair of top guns recruited from within the vast Hawker-Siddeley Group joined Rogers and Cooper-Slipper. These two chief test pilots from England couldn't have been more dissimilar.

Soft-spoken and thoughtful, Jimmy Orrell was on loan from Avro, where he had been responsible for testing the Avro Lancaster, York, and Tudor. His background as both an ex-RAF and Imperial Airways pilot was mainly with large transports, but he also had recent experience with jet aircraft. When the Jetliner emerged from assembly on July 25, 1949, Orrell was poised to become one of the immortals in the annals of test flight. By a trick of fate, he missed his opportunity by scant days when an extended engine test accidentally caused the nacelles that covered the jet exhausts to collapse. While the nacelles were being replaced, word came that Avro's great rival, the de Havilland Comet, had made a short test hop.

Orrell stoically continued his work with his very careful and methodical approach. He carried out 16 test flights with the C102 Jetliner, helping to establish the credentials of the program. The only mishap in testing occurred during the second flight, when he was setting up the prototype for a landing approach and the undercarriage refused to budge. Flight Engineer Bill Baker strenuously ratcheted the emergency gear-down handle in the cockpit to no avail. In his energetic thrashing, Baker did not even notice he had broken several ribs. Frantic efforts by the engineering staff on the ground could not produce any solutions. Jim Floyd, the chief engineer, asked the pilot-in-command if he had any last thoughts on the subject. Without a moment's hesitation, Jimmy Orrell intoned drily over the intercom, "Our Father, which art in heaven ..."

While the Avro officials on the ground sweated out the next moments, dreading the thought of losing their precious prototype, Orrell coolly set up four separate approaches, each time testing a combination of speeds, flap settings, and controls. Then, drifting in on a crosswind approach, Orrell put the Jetliner down on the grass next to Malton Airport's east-west runway. He eased the aircraft onto the damp grass in a nose-up skid, sliding gracefully to a halt. When Floyd and the other engineers examined the aircraft, they were amazed that only minimal damage had occurred to the underside. The popular pilot and his wife made the most of their three-month stay in Canada, appearing at various functions. Jimmy was constantly touted as the saviour of the company, an accolade he laughed off easily.

Shortly after Orrell left Canada, the mercurial Squadron Leader William A. "Bill" Waterton descended on Malton. If anyone had an image in mind of the stereotypical British test pilot, complete with derring-do, swagger, and handlebar moustache, Waterton fit the picture. That he was an expatriate Canadian from Camrose, Alberta, wasn't initially evident. He had made his mark as a wartime RAF fighter pilot, instructor, and test pilot before attaining worldwide notice as a member of the RAF's World Air Speed Record team, flying the Gloster Meteor (616 mph on September 7, 1946). Later in the same year, Waterton set the Paris-London speed record.

At Gloster Aircraft, Waterton was involved in development work on the Meteor, the RAF's first operational jet fighter. He also gained recognition as a skilled aerobatic performer in wringing out Gloster products at the prestigious Farnborough Air Display.

When the company embarked on a revolutionary design, the delta wing Javelin, Waterton and other Gloster test pilots were openly at odds with the Design Office. Although his tirades could have been dismissed as prima-donna behaviour, Waterton recognized the design had inherently deadly traits, including a deep stall and vicious pitch-up characteristics. The Javelin nearly killed him when part of the tail section broke off during a high-speed run. Only incredible skill combined with an amazing stroke of luck saved his life. This combination would once more come to his rescue at Avro Canada.

After making the hop from Toronto to Boston in an Avro CF-100 prototype at an average cruise speed of 575 mph, Bill Waterton and his back-seater, Bruce Warren, landed at Logan Field on August 30, 1950. As soon as Waterton arrived, he supervised preparations to have his aircraft, #18102 — the second CF-100 Mk.1 and resplendent in its paint scheme of gloss black with white lightning stripes — ready for the upcoming air show. The USAF annual reunion held that weekend would bring General Hoyt Vandenburg, chief of air staff, to Boston. The Avro CF-100 was a contender in an American tactical fighter/bomber competition and the Boston Air Show would be an opportunity to showcase its capabilities.

To Waterton's dismay, the air show committee refused to allow aerobatics at the civil airport. All flying exhibitions had to take place over the Atlantic. Waterton knew that flying far out over water would not give the spectators much of a show, but he had spotted a tiny bay on the north side of the airfield. When he brought the matter up with the air show executive, Waterton vigorously set out his case that his demonstration would be over water. Given permission to confine his display to this area, he worked up a tight routine.

Waterton began his performance by blasting off in a full-throttle climb. Unfortunately, his takeoff was right in the middle of General Vandenburg's speech. The CF-100 display caught the general's attention. The aircraft's rate of climb and manoeuvrability looked spectacular in the hands of an expert like Waterton.

Ever the showman, Waterton pushed the limits of the prototype CF-100 further. With the aircraft just above the runway, flaps down, nose-up and hovering just above stall speed, he hit the throttles. Then, in the parlance of the airman, hours and hours of boredom were, indeed, punctuated by moments of sheer terror: the starboard engine stalled! His "dicey-doo" had left him at low altitude with virtually no speed and flaps extended. Pushing down with all his might, he nursed the rumbling, shaking CF-100 along until he could ease the fighter to a height sufficient to raise the flaps and carry out a single-engine landing. His actions saved both his life and the aircraft.

In the CF-100 program, Waterton passionately took on the job of shepherding the prototypes from ground test to flight status. His admirers spoke of his enthusiasm and commitment, while detractors were wary of Waterton's bravado and his tendency to exaggerate the potential of the prototype. Mario Pesando from Flight Engineering was especially concerned. "I hold Waterton responsible for many of the delays and improvements that should have been accomplished during the fifteen months that he was at Avro Canada," he said, "needless, we didn't get along and he misled the company about the maximum speed of the CF-100 ..."

Regardless of the emotions he evoked, Bill Waterton identified a potentially fatal flaw in the CF-100 wing spar and worked hard to affect a remedy. He had the support of Don Rogers and John Frost, but his controversial tenure ended before the prototypes were modified. His replacement was a noted RCAF test pilot, Flight Lieutenant Bruce "Duke" Warren, whose time as chief pilot of the CF-100 ended before it really began. Warren and his observer, Robert Ostrander, mysteriously died in a crash on April 5, 1951, while flying the second CF-100 prototype. A small tube from Warren's helmet later found in his desk at the plant may have likely sealed his fate. Like most pilots, he had cleaned his own oxygen mask that day. The grim scenario of the pilot passing out at height when his oxygen mask failed matched reports from a Trans-Canada Airline crew who had witnessed a black jet in a vertical dive straight into the ground. They were the first Avro Canada flight crew to give their lives, but not the last.

In November 2000, Mark Matthys, a tobacco farmer who lived near the crash site at Mount Brydges, Ontario recovered a small scrap of the cockpit frame. Scalloping the mud under the metal, he exposed a skull fragment. For years, sheet metal shards had turned up throughout a large debris field circling the impact crater. Even a smashed watch bearing the designation "Avro" and a serial number were found in a wooded area near the farm. Matthys contacted DOT (Department of Transport) investigators, who thoroughly combed the area, turning up more remnants of the CF-100 accident. On April 5, 2001, the farmer placed a wooden cross and flag at the crash site and, according to Matthys, "on the anniversary date for the rest of his life, he would commemorate the passing of these gallant fliers."

Chapter 5

The Greatest of Them All

The morning showers had not persisted and by mid-afternoon the sky brightened over Farnborough, England. The assigned time for Jan Zurakowski's flight demonstration of the Avro CF-100 Mk.4b fighter was 1345 hours on Monday, September 5, 1955. It was the first "trade day" of the world-class event. The stringent schedule of the SBAC (Society of British Aircraft Constructors) air show required that each aircraft take off within 30 seconds of its designated time. In order to ensure that "Zura" did not miss his slot, he was strapped in with the twin Orenda engines ticking over.

John F. Painter, the Avro Canada service representative in charge of the exhibition team of pilots and ground crew, was listening to the proceedings over a headset. Without warning, the organizers requested the Avro CF-100 to move into position, a full 12 minutes ahead of schedule. Reacting immediately, Zurakowski swung the fighter onto the taxiway and punched both engines into full military thrust.

Streaking down the main runway, the CF-100 literally jumped into the air with Zurakowski simultaneously hitting the undercarriage switch, raising the gear as soon as the tires left the tarmac. Pointing the nose straight up, he wrenched the CF-100 into a vertical climb, but reduced power to idle on both power plants. The massive fighter sat momentarily transfixed in the sky, then it slid downward gracefully tail first. After a few hundred feet, Zura pushed over, pointed the nose to the ground, and swooped away, a few feet above the runway. Over 100,000 spectators stared gap-mouthed and wide-eyed.

The first to react were the usually composed air show announcers. One blurted out, "It's another Zurabatic!" harkening back to the time that Jan Zurakowski had demonstrated an entirely new manoeuvre at the 1951 Farnborough Air Show. His display that year had featured a cartwheel that had seemingly suspended a Gloster Meteor as it pirouetted above the crowd. The aerobatic manoeuvre had been appropriately dubbed the "Zurabatic Cartwheel."

During the course of the three-day 1955 Farnborough flying program, Zurakowski demonstrated a number of tail-slides, sometimes with a "falling leaf" added to the routine. This delicate manoeuvre made the heavy fighter flutter to the

Avro test pilots: (l-r) Peter Cope, Chris Pike, Janusz Zurakowski, Mike Cooper-Slipper, Don Rogers, Stan Haswell, Glen Lynes.

ground in a series of near-stalls. It looked exactly like a leaf gently rising and falling as if caught by the wind on its slow descent earthward.

To the astonishment of the audience, Zura added one more incredible aerial trick to his performance. On the second flying day, he took off normally, then rolled the CF-100 on its back and hit the undercarriage button. With the gear retracting downward, Zura twisted the aircraft back to normal and roared away. Geoffrey Norris from the RAF Flying Review described his performance as "impossible, of course, but not for the Great Zura."

Fred Smye, vice president and general manager of Avro Aircraft Limited, wrote Zurakowski personally to thank him for a "magnificent performance ... the highlight of the show and a demonstration of flying skill which will long be remembered by those who were fortunate enough to be present." The exploits of Avro's most famous test pilot put the company in the world's headlines again.

Jan Zurakowski, a Polish officer and RAF war veteran, was fast making a name for himself as not only a proficient test pilot but also as a superb aerobatic flier. Born in Ryzawka, Russia, on September 12, 1914, Janusz Zurakowski and his family immigrated to a newly emerged Poland in the turbulent years after World War One. As youths, Janusz and his older brother, Bronislaw, were interested in aviation and yearned to fly. Janusz' reward for winning a first prize in a model aircraft competition was a flight in a elderly biplane at the Lublin Flying club. From his first exhilarating moments in the air, Janusz' life course had been set.

By the 1930s, after learning to fly on gliders, he became a fighter pilot at a time when Poland faced its greatest adversity. Posted as a sub-lieutenant to 161 Squadron, flying the PZL P-11c on the frontier, he later became an instructor at the Central Flying School in Deblin. On September 2, 1939,

Zurakowski was at the controls of a PZL P-7 training aircraft pitted against Luftwaffe Dornier Do-17 bombers. Although he damaged one of the raiders, his first combat was inconclusive. The brave but desperate missions flown by the Polish Air Force ended dramatically on September 17, when the Soviet Union attacked Poland on its southern flank.

With the imminent fall of Poland, Zurakowski and other instructors were ordered to take delivery of British fighters and bombers in Rumania. After being briefly interned, Zurakowski, along with other surviving military personnel, began an odyssey that took him to France and finally England to continue his fight. As a part of an advance unit sent to the RAF, he joined the RAF Volunteer Reserve as a pilot officer. Flying a Spitfire in the Battle of Britain, Zura, as he was known by his British compatriots, became a skilled and deadly fighter pilot with numerous victories. Transferring to a succession of Polish squadrons, he was promoted to squadron leader before his selection to train as a test pilot.

Graduating from the Empire Test Pilots School in March 1944, along with fellow classmate Jimmy Orrell, Zurakowski was subsequently appointed to the Aircraft & Armament Experimental Establishment (A&AEE) at Boscombe Down. During the Boscombe Down period, Jan Zurakowski emerged as a highly proficient test pilot, flying all the contemporary British and Allied aircraft. In testing the superlative DH Hornet, he discovered he could almost tumble through the sky in a cartwheel manoeuvre. His aerobatics in the Martin-

Baker Mk.5 fighter are regarded as the most impressive piston-engined routine ever performed at the Farnborough Air Show.

In 1947, Zurakowski joined Gloster Aircraft Company as a development test pilot flying the Meteor, the RAF's first jet. During his Gloster years, he set world speed records, flew the first high-speed aerobatic photography flights, and his dazzling aerial demonstrations at Farnborough were in all of the world's headlines. Zura is one of the few pilots to have invented an aerobatic manoeuvre. At home with slide rules and graphs as much as he was in the cockpit, he utilized the unique jet engine placement of the Gloster Meteor to create a "cartwheel," a manoeuvre that had originated on the Hornet. By throttling one engine back and pouring power into the other engine, he seemed to gyrate in place above the startled crowd in the 1951 Farnborough Air Show.

After testing the new Gloster Javelin in 1952, Zurakowski wrote to Peter R. Cope, the new test pilot for the CF-100, inquiring about the Avro Canada operation. Cope immediately counselled him to come to Canada. He joked later that he had actually recruited his own boss.

Following Avro Canada's enthusiastic response to his inquiries, Zurakowski resigned at Gloster and, with his young family in tow, he came to Canada as a test pilot for the CF-100. After a long flight across the Atlantic, the Zurakowskis must have been buoyed by the warm reception they received at Malton. Waiting at the airport was a delegation of Polish-

Canadians, alerted by a veterans' association of the pending arrival of a famous Polish hero. The next few days were a blur of news conferences and meetings on top of the usual business of unpacking and setting up a new home.

Once Zurakowski checked in with the Flight Operations Department, he fit in easily with his new colleagues. Reuniting with old friend Peter Cope made the transition even smoother.

It was soon evident that Zurakowski was an extraordinary test pilot. Co-workers noted his careful and methodical approach to problems. Fred Smye, vice president of Avro Aircraft, and Jim Floyd, head of engineering, were ardent fans. Floyd later remarked that, "in addition to being a superb test pilot, arguably the best acrobatic pilot in the world, Jan also took an engineering approach to flying and 'coaxed' an aircraft to the limit of its performance, often taking his mount beyond the accepted limits ... Jan's philosophy was based on his feeling that, should a service pilot find himself in trouble if he inadvertently took the aircraft outside of its specified performance, the procedures for safe recovery had to established."

Nearly everyone who had contact with Zurakowski had a story to tell. His boss, Don Rogers, remembered that Zura would know the weight of an aircraft by instinct. A particular test involved loading up a CF-100. One glance at the set-up and Zurakowski announced the weight. The technicians then weighed the aircraft and shook their heads in wonderment; Zura was bang on. Rogers never doubted it for a moment.

When Flight Engineering began to recognize that Zura established his own test routines to explore the capabilities of the CF-100, a request was sent for a tail-slide manoeuvre. The test pilot studied the note on the assignment sheet carefully then pronounced that it wasn't possible. "But we know you have been practising tail-slides all week!" He laughed. "Ah, but that was for me. For you, tail-slides — no good." He was right; service pilots never needed that kind of air show trick. The tail-slide, however, remained in the repertoire of a master like Zurakowski.

Roy Combley flew as Zura's flight observer on countless tests. He was in awe at the precision and control that Zura maintained throughout a flight, declaring, "I have never flown with a smoother pilot." When the aileron controls failed during one flight, Combley marvelled that Zura effortlessly brought their CF-100 prototype in with completely locked ailerons. He mused that no other pilot could have accomplished that feat.

Zurakowski's mechanical knowledge was also uncanny. Shop foreman Bob Johnson told the story of how Zurakowski "pancaked" in with a collapsed landing gear and insisted that the aircraft had retracted the main gear on its own. Mechanics couldn't find the fault, but after a vigorous slap on the fuselage, lo and behold, the CF-100 on the test stand raised its gear.

Chris Pike, a fellow test pilot, would regale his friends with how Zurakowski did the customary "walk-around" that all pilots took before flight. Zura would just touch a recess and announce that a part was missing, and he would be right. When Peter Cope and other pilots couldn't determine the reason for one of the test aircraft always dipping a wing in flight, Zurakowski stared at the wing and then produced a straightedge ruler. A quick look at the ruler showed a gap between the leading edge and the rest of the wing. Sure enough, after the crooked leading edge of the offending wing was filled in, the aircraft flew perfectly.

One practice that Zurakowski had brought from his years with the Meteor was the formation aerobatic flying that had propelled the Gloster products onto newspaper headlines worldwide. His friend and Gloster company photographer, Russell Adams, had come along on many test flights to take some amazing aerial photographs of the Meteor. In Avro Canada's company photographer, Hugh Mackechnie, Zurakowski recognized a similar kindred spirit of innovation and adventure.

After talking Mackechnie into the back cockpit of a CF-100, Zurakowski showed him a dizzying array of aerial tricks. When he had trained a number of other test pilots to fly precision formation, he then led them into aerobatic routines. Zurakowski invariably flew the camera ship. It was his job to place the photographer in the exact location for a spectacular shot. He never failed. The Avro public relations department received a bevy of beautiful aerial photographs, courtesy of Zurakowski.

Zura's sense of fun was also legendary, specifically, his continual threats of resignation. He would instruct a secretary to prepare a formal letter. Each time his boss, Don Rogers, found the letter in his in-box, he flipped it over and brushed it aside. When another little irritant cropped up, he knew that Zura would again be dropping off a resignation. On the occasion of Zurakowski's penultimate tiff with flight engineering, Rogers turned his resignation letter over to find another resignation letter on the other side. Looking up, he spotted Zurakowski at an adjoining window between their offices, smiling broadly.

Chapter 6
Pushing the Envelope

Upon his arrival in 1952, the first task set for Jan Zurakowski at Avro Aircraft was to wring out the latest version of the Avro CF-100. His test flight confirmed that there was still a great deal of development work to be done. Zura took the aircraft up to altitude and, using the pilots' notes, recognized that the limiting .85 Mach number could easily be exceeded.

When Zurakowski approached Jim Chamberlin in the Design Office, Jim reassured him that the CF-100 would be stable up to its limits. Zura then asked what would happen if a service pilot accidentally flew faster. The generally held opinion in engineering was that the fighter would be uncontrollable. Despite these warnings, Zura was determined to find out if the CF-100 was safe at high-speed.

With the backing of engineer Mario Pesando, Zurakowski began exploring the upper ranges of the flight envelope. Diving from 40,000 feet, the CF-100 accelerated steadily until a slight buffeting announced the onset of phenomena of compressibility. The build-up of air pressure at the speed of sound was once thought to present a solid barrier that caused many piston-engined fighters to break up. Zura looked down in amazement as he watched his Machmeter needle creep up to and then move past Mach 1.

A deafening sonic boom struck the Ontario countryside. Janusz Zurakowski was one of a handful of pilots around the world to achieve supersonic flight. When Pesando informed Jim Floyd that Zurakowski had just flown past the sound barrier, the two conspired to reveal the capabilities of the CF-100 in a dramatic way. Ushering Chamberlin and the rest of the engineering staff into a room equipped with a radio link to the control tower, Floyd asked the question again: "What would happen if a pilot flew past the aircraft's posted limits?" He listened to the usual dire warnings and then excused himself to fiddle with the radio controls. With a flick of the dial, Zurakowski's voice filled the room, and huge double sonic bangs shook the building. Floyd and Pesando shared a meaningful glance. Zurakowski had shown the "iron in his blood."

Proving the CF-100 was a safe and reliable aircraft even at supersonic speeds was one of Zurakowski's primary imperatives as a test pilot. With this accomplishment, he found that he was at odds with the Design Office. A transonic replacement of the CF-100 had been proposed, but now the company was forced to abandon the project. Zurakowski continued to take production CF-100 aircraft through the development phases, setting the stage for the fighters to enter operational service in April 1953.

Whenever safety was at stake, unorthodox methods were sometimes employed to make a point. When the company insisted that the CF-100's new heating and air conditioning system was adequate, Zurakowski took up a flight observer for a lengthy test of the system. Without telling George Shaw, the engineer aboard for the test, Zura had put on extra sweaters and two pairs of thermal underwear. After cruising at high-altitude for an hour, he glanced back to see Shaw had nearly frozen stiff. The poor observer had to be lifted out of the cockpit like a slab of frozen meat. Engineering quickly modified the heater after that.

As he had done before in England, Zura showed the capabilities of the aircraft he tested by putting on spectacular aerobatic shows. One of the most memorable displays took place on the occasion of the visit to the plant by legendary British war hero, Brigadier General Bernard Montgomery. He asked for a demonstration of the latest CF-100, but was surprised when Zurakowski did one of his customary "sneaky" routines. As the visiting party of dignitaries assembled near the airfield, Zura swept around a nearby hangar in a knife-edge pass just a few feet over their heads. A photograph of the scene clearly shows the group scattering with only Montgomery bravely facing the onrushing jet fighter. The general later applauded Zurakowski for his audacious performance.

The day-to-day testing of the CF-100 continued through progressive versions and soon required additional staff in development test flying. Once again, Avro Canada turned to England, where Wladyslaw Jan "Spud" Potocki was testing the mighty Avro Vulcan bomber at Avro (U.K.). He had been associated with Zurakowski throughout the war years when they had both served in 306 Squadron. While Zurakowski was the commanding officer, Potocki had only been a sergeant-pilot, a fact Zura would bring up good-naturedly from time to time. Potocki had followed a similar career path, proceeding from RAF wartime service to the Empire Test Pilots' School. When he was recruited to come to Canada, the price he demanded for his services was relatively high. Zura had again tendered his resignation in jest at the supposed indignity of Potocki's higher salary. All the pilots in Avro Canada would receive a commiserate salary increase.

An additional team of RCAF test pilots was assigned to the factory. Squadron Leader Ken Owen commanded a detachment that included Flight Lieutenants Jack Woodman, Reg Kersey and N. "Norm" Ronaasen. Woodman was the chief test pilot at the RCAF's Central Experimental and Proving Establishment before joining as an acceptance pilot at the Avro plant. An incomparable flier, he was later slated to be the first Canadian selected for astronaut training. "Flying with Don Rogers and the Avro team was an honour for me," he recalled in a 1978 interview, "and I thoroughly enjoyed the four years I spent at Avro. I mentioned Zurakowski being the best test pilot I have ever known; the rest of the team, and all the Avro troops, were of the same calibre."

His ground crew knew how thorough Zurakowski could be. Whenever an aircraft had a "snag," it was noted on the flight report. Zurakowski's reports were always meticulous and if he wrote "NNS" on the margin, it was his subtle reminder to Engineering that there were "no new snags," but the problems already identified had not yet been fixed. Invariably, Zurakowski would find every "gremlin" that lurked in an aircraft and ensure that the aircraft would be safe to fly for others.

Safety for aircrews was Zurakowski's principal concern, and one battle he had with Engineering revealed that testing could prove the difference between life and death. Ejecting from a damaged CF-100 had to provide a measure of safety and reliability for both pilot and back seater. Zura was not convinced that the standard operating procedures or equipment were up to the job. It was his belief that the canopy would not detach properly and he flew countless tests, blowing canopies off their mounts until he was satisfied.

Ejection tests with dummies had not shown enough, so Zurakowski insisted that live demonstrations take place. A Martin-Baker representative flew with him and ejected out of the back seat, but Zura was still not assured that the ejection procedures were sound. Peter Cope's experience with a flight observer showed that the man in the back seat could not move his hands above his head to grasp the ejection handles on the seat. The rush of air around the back cockpit had pinned the observer's hands behind his head. Adding a small windscreen to the rear cockpit finally eliminated that problem.

Zurakowski's concerns about ejection from a CF-100 were not misplaced. On August 23, 1954, during the testing of a centrally mounted rocket pack, Zurakowski and his flight engineer, John Hiebert, came face-to-face with a deadly situation. High over the Ajax, Ontario, test range, an explosion crippled their test aircraft. Zurakowski initiated emergency procedures and ordered his observer to eject.

When a second explosion rippled through the airplane, Zurakowski ejected. Immediately he felt a searing pain in his right leg. The parachute blossomed above him, but he could tell that his ankle was broken. Landing painfully in a farmer's field seconds before the CF-100 slammed into the ground, Zura looked around, but he couldn't see a second parachute. Onlookers and police soon identified the crash site and relayed the message to him that his observer hadn't made it. From his hospital bed, he learned that Hiebert had been trapped in the rear cockpit.

Later tests showed that the face blind that was pulled down to begin the ejection process had snagged. Avro engineer Ron Page found in testing that he could not release the blind when it was tugged slightly off centre. It may have been this fault that had doomed Hiebert aboard the stricken aircraft.

Changing ejection procedures and adding release handles mounted low on the seat prevented this tragedy from recurring. A sheared lock-pin on Zurakowski's seat had resulted in his seat being propelled sideways, slamming his right leg on the canopy rail as he left the aircraft. His broken ankle healed properly and Zura returned to flying, ever cognizant of the dangers of test flying. The difficulty in ejecting out of a CF-100 would claim the life of one more test pilot.

Glen Lynes was an accomplished test pilot who had recently joined the Production group. His background as an Empire Test Pilots' School graduate, as well as his extensive experience in both the RAF and RCAF, had elevated him to the position of backup to Zurakowski in air displays. He had accompanied Zura to England for the 1955 Farnborough show and stayed on the continent to conduct aerial demonstrations for NATO (North Atlantic Treaty Organization) squadrons about to receive the CF-100.

On a routine test flight in one of the highly modified CF-100s, Lynes got into trouble when he entered an inverted spin. He had "punched out," but everything had gone horribly wrong. Lynes never pulled the rip-chord on his parachute, crashing to the earth in front of Avro test pilots Stan Haswell and Chris Pike, who were waiting in line to take off. As it turned out, Lynes had ejected straight through the canopy and had broken his neck. The addition of spikes on the ejection seat would allow CF-100 pilots and aircrew in the future to eject through the plexiglas. During their next get-together, Don Rogers' band of pilots each hoisted a drink in Lynes' memory and, in their customary way, put the death out of their minds. It was simply the nature of their business.

In 1955, Jan Zurakowski became the chief development test pilot at Avro Aircraft Limited, taking over all the experimental programs. The next project that Zurakowski would undertake, however, would push the limits of aerodynamics and aircraft performance into completely uncharted territory. Zura was named as the pilot of the Avro Arrow.

Chapter 7 Genesis of the Arrow

Alarms bells clanged shrilly at the 138th Fighter Interceptor Squadron ready-room. The ADC (Air Defence Command) radar station at Syracuse, New York, had detected an intruder. Lieutenant Colonel Curtis J. Irwin, commanding officer of the Air National Guard Squadron, was already sprinting out to one of the two Lockheed F-94B Starfire fighters kept on alert status. Gordon W. Simonds, 2nd Lieutenant, was strapping up in the second fighter. The scramble had "the boys from Syracuse" vectored to Lake Ontario to intercept a fast-moving target estimated at over Mach 1. Irwin's radar operator called out. "It's gone, Sir! The blip just disappeared off the screen."

The target was indeed gone. FFM-8 had already impacted

and disintegrated in the cold waters of Lake Ontario, 120 kilometres away. The one-eighth-scale magnesium alloy model painted white with a red rudder and a black number "8," had reached Mach 1.7 in its brief 40-second life on November 6, 1956. FFM-8 was one of a series of free-flight test models of the Avro Arrow that were launched from the Point Petrie, Ontario, test site. The scale model had been mounted on a Nike rocket booster for its flight. Each model had two FM transmitters that provided telemetry to a ground station. FFM-8 had relayed a burst of data providing readings on the lateral stability of the model before its demise.

Since the aerodynamic configuration of the Avro Arrow had to be determined prior to production, an elaborate set of tests had been conducted with scale models. Most of the models were destined for wind tunnel and water tests, but flight test results were necessary to verify drag coefficients and the longitudinal and lateral stability of the proposed supersonic fighter. Eleven free-flight tests would confirm that the aerodynamic design of the CF-105 would meet every expectation.

The Avro CF-105 Arrow was a steel, titanium, and aluminium wonder that represented the cutting-edge aeronautical technology of the 1950s.

To even the unschooled observer, the sleek giant looked every bit a world-beater. The powerful, delta-winged interceptor was designed to fly faster and higher than anything in the skies. It combined all of the latest cutting-edge technology in aeronautics, electronics, jet engines and weaponry into a streamlined dart. To see it fly was breath-taking; even today, few aircraft are its equal. Its origins dated back to Avro's 1948 research program for an advanced supersonic interceptor. It would be a weapons system, in the words of Jim Floyd, "capable of long-range operation by day or by night, in any weather ... particularly suited to defend Canada's Northern frontier."

Both Floyd and Jim Chamberlin were members of the "think tank" that initiated studies when the RCAF requested a follow-up for the CF-100. Avro Canada's Long-Range Projects group designed the CF-103, incorporating the latest swept-wing technology wherein a sharply angled wing proved to be superior at high speeds. A CF-100 fuselage married to swept-wing and tail surfaces was considered promising enough to proceed to mock-up stage by 1951. However, the modest performance increase of this design merely nudged the contemporary CF-100 airframe into transonic territory. Even before Zurakowski flew supersonically, the CF-103 was abandoned in favour of more revolutionary concepts.

An RCAF review of current fighters in the United Kingdom and the United States, conducted by Wing Commander Ray Foottit, had resulted in *RCAF Operational Requirement ORI/1-63,* issued in November 1952. The report even investigated projects on the drawing boards in an effort to determine if any design existed that could meet the stringent RCAF requirements for an advanced supersonic interceptor.

On the basis of the April 1953, *Specification AIR 7-3*, the RCAF interceptor of the future would be able to:

- Function in Canada's harsh Arctic environment
- Have two engines for safety
- Carry an advanced weapon system
- Be crewed by a pilot and a navigator
- Operate from a 6000-foot runway
- Be capable of accelerating to Mach 1.5
- Manoeuvre at 50,000 feet while pulling 2G, without loss of speed or altitude
- Have a range of 600 nautical miles

Avro's Preliminary Design Office considered the RCAF requirements carefully, laying out a series of new designs named C-104 and C-105. The restructured Advanced Projects Group was given the task of designing an advanced fighter. Floyd and Chamberlin, as group leaders, considered a diverse number of design elements including both rocket and turbojet engines, and swept-wing and delta wing configurations before submitting a final proposal. Compared to the conventional CF-100, the C-105 outlined in *Design Study Report P/C-105/1* was a revolutionary design. Powered by either two Rolls-Royce RB-106 or Curtiss-Wright turbojet YJ67W engines, fitted with afterburners, the C-105's delta wing and sleek "coke-bottle" contours promised incredible performance, exceeding even the RCAF's demanding specifications. An all-missile armament housed internally along with an advanced avionics and weapons targeting system complemented the state-of-the art design. With military backing, the Canadian government funded the development of two C-105 prototype aircraft in December 1953.

Three major factors had to be considered in the C-105 from the outset: weight, performance, and installation features. Due to mission requirements, in terms of fuel capacity and weapons load, a large aircraft was necessary. In order to meet the targeted speed and altitude, the design team chose a thin delta wing with recognized optimal lift and drag characteristics. Using a high-mounted wing and "buried" weapons provided a streamlined shape, but limited stowage of the undercarriage. The design of a complex main gear by Dowty Equipment that retracted into the wing solved that problem. A careful harmonizing of the main systems also led to an effective maintenance and servicing design: a weapons bay that could be easily removed on the ground, and engines that could be pulled out of the rear fuselage in minutes.

The technology incorporated in the design would involve the latest advances in aerodynamics, electronics, power plants, weapons, and avionics. It would be the first aircraft to incorporate titanium in critical structural areas. Many new innovations were needed in order to produce the components, from autoclaves to giant stamping machinery. The anticipated performance would require new materials that would withstand the heat generated at Mach 2. Control surfaces were "fly-by-wire," the first use of electric and electronic systems rather than the usual mechanical systems. The powerful IBM 704 had been employed in the design process. The test aircraft would be loaded with electronic signalling devices, known today as black boxes. These elements of the design would be integrated seamlessly into the final configuration.

Engines, weapons, and avionics on the project would not come together as easily. Difficulties involving the initial choice of advanced jet engines had prompted a private-venture program at Orenda to design a new engine. Abandonment of a Canadian-designed "Velvet Glove" missile meant reliance on a new Douglas Sparrow missile and a RCA "Astra" avionics package, both untested and unproven systems. According to the design dictates of Jim Floyd, a radically new aircraft should rely on conventional and proven engines and systems. But now he was embarking on a revolutionary fighter that involved new engines, weapons, and avionics — a volatile mix.

During this period, under the new leadership of Crawford Gordon Jr., A.V. Roe Canada became a beehive of activity. With Avro Aircraft Ltd. stepping up manufacture of the CF-100, and Avro Orenda Engines engaged in large-scale production of the Orenda series of engines, expansion of both divisions was required. There were over 15,000 employees at Malton, while an equal number of jobs were found in the over 400 sub-contractors involved in maintaining a parts supply.

The Hawker-Siddeley Group, aware of the success of its subsidiary, began to invest heavily in Canada. By 1954, A.V. Roe Canada had diversified into shipping, steel products, truck and bus transportation, iron and coal mining, railway rolling stock, computers and electronics, and even purchased majority ownership of another aviation company — Can-Car. Huge enterprises such as Canadian Steel Improvement Limited and the Dominion Steel and Coal Corporation (Dosco) were also added to A.V. Roe Canada's empire. In direct or majority control of over 44 companies, with total employee ranks over 50,000, and annual sales of $450 million, A.V. Roe Canada was the third-largest corporation in Canada. Fittingly, the new company motto was "The Next Big Step."

At Avro Aircraft, the next big step was centred on its newest aviation design, the C-105, which was soon to be designated the CF-105 and acquire the name "The Arrow." Sadly, the first great project of the aviation firm had wound to an end. Relegated to use as a camera platform for aerial photography and with no prospects for future orders, the Jetliner was scrapped. The destruction came at an unfortunate time. Its great rival, the Comet, had been withdrawn from service as the result of a series of catastrophic failures, while the Boeing 707 had still not entered regular service. The last vestiges of Avro's aspirations as a manufacturer of airliners fizzled with the termination of Jetliner program.

Avro was now banking its future on the CF-105 Arrow

project. Excitement rippled through every department at Avro Aircraft and Orenda Engines. This was not just another aircraft project; the Avro Arrow began to take on a life of its own. Employees vied for the honour of working on its development. Even "the Great Zura" was flattered when he was assigned to the Arrow team. And what a team it was!

Avro assembled the "best of the best" in every area. Led by the charismatic and enigmatic Crawford Gordon and bolstered by his able right-hand man, Fred Smye, the management team made some crucial decisions. Chief Engineer James Floyd personally took charge of the design. Jim Chamberlin led the aerodynamic research while Wilf Farrance, a young genius, took over the internal systems design, with an eye to the new art and science termed "ergonomics." Harvey R. Smith, head of Manufacturing, developed a new system based on the "Cook-Craigie Plan," which shortened the length of production time, eliminating a prototype stage. Charles Grinyer at Orenda began work on an advanced new engine, the mighty "Iroquois," which would eventually be earmarked for the Arrow.

Engineering and technical positions were critical in the design of the CF-105 Arrow. One of the initiatives taken by William Dickie, head of Industrial Relations, was to recruit heavily in Canada, the United States, and the United Kingdom. For years, top-flight graduates of universities, technical colleges, and trade schools could expect a call from Avro Canada. One of Dickie's most important operatives was

Elwy Yost, who set up shop in the shadow of the great English aerospace companies. Scores of British families would make their way to Canada during the 1950s due to the Avro Arrow project.

The village of Malton and the surrounding townships around Toronto became "company towns" as employees took up residence nearby. A government-sponsored Defence Workers' Homes scheme created over 1000 houses in a Malton subdivision. These modest bungalows were priced between $7000 and $10,000 at a 3 percent interest rate. Avro sponsored a payroll deduction plan to purchase homes for over 1500 staff. Avro families lived throughout southern Ontario. Over 7000 resided in Metro Toronto, and more than 1000 employees each lived in Brampton, Chinguacousy, and Peel County. Acton, Bolton, Caledon, Georgetown, Milton, Orangeville, Port Credit, and Streetsville each had 200 Avroite residents.

Avro functioned like a homegrown operation in an era when the T. Eaton Company was seen as a model business. The tightly knit community of Avro Canada had from its very beginnings looked after its employees' well being. Don Lingwood, the director of recreation, organized male and female baseball, basketball, football, soccer, and hockey teams that played in industrial leagues in Toronto. The Avro Recreation Club eventually extended to include arts, bowling, bridge, crafts, darts, film, fishing, gardening, golf, ham-radio, model-building, record, rocketry, sailing, sports-car, swimming, target-shooting, theatre, and drama clubs. A series of open houses and picnics sponsored by the company served to bring Avro families together. The picnics and Christmas parties hosted by Crawford Gordon himself were so well attended that they had to be shifted to locations such as the Maple Leaf Gardens and the CNE Coliseum.

Social conscience was a strong element in the Avro operation. Employee benefits were varied and included a group insurance and dental plan. The company hired over 300 handicapped individuals, a progressive move, even by today's standards. Riveters John Little and Charles McKenzie, who worked together as a team, had no problem with the incredible din of the factory — they were both deaf mutes. Avro was also an industry leader in affirmative hiring practices that did not discriminate against a candidate's background or race. When Avro employee, Jim Marshall, was refused entry into the Lakewood Golf Club because he was black, Avro cancelled its annual golf tournament at the club.

Avro made a concerted effort to reward innovation and initiative. When machinist Norm Austring fashioned a new jig to speed CF-100 production, he was immediately promoted to junior engineer. The Avro Scholarship Committee provided an annual Engineering and Science Scholarship to the children of Avro employees. The company also maintained a number of training schools for trades and specialties. In January 1958, trainee Claude Sherwood was one of eleven draftsmen who graduated from a 19-week course at the Avro Training School as a junior engineer, after which he was assigned to the Design Office. Training at colleges and universities was likewise provided for junior engineers. Peter Armitage would complete his Masters in Engineering at the College of Aeronautics in Cranfield, England.

If hard times befell individuals or communities, Avro employees were quick to react. When James Kirkpatrick passed away suddenly, leaving behind a wife and three infants, not only did the Employees' Welfare Fund contribute cash and mortgage payments to help the family move into their partly constructed home, colleagues in the Assembly Bay picked up his toolbox and sold it. The money they raised was used to finish the house. When Hurricane Hazel carved its murderous path across Toronto and southern Ontario in October 1954, Avro workers were there to drive ambulances and emergency vehicles and to provide relief by taking in people who had been left destitute. Long lines of Avro employees queued to donate blood. A record response by Avro employees to Red Cross Society appeals for blood donors continued until 1959.

The giant complex of Avro Aircraft Limited and the neighbouring Orenda Engine plant included a hospital, security force, fire department, training facilities, and water and sewage systems, as well as services such as cafeteria/restaurants, and mail, photographic, and printing/publication departments. Work went on 24 hours a day, 7 days a week, in shifts. The largest traffic jams in Canada occurred as Avro employees arrived for shift changes.

There was a unique atmosphere at Avro. Zurakowski once recalled that an older gentleman had stated proudly that he was an Avro employee and then engaged him in a long dialogue about test flying. Only at the end of the conversation did Zurakowski ask him what he did at the company. "I work in the mail room!" was the response. Regardless of where Avro people worked, they were proud of what they did.

The future for Avro and its employees, who proudly called themselves "Avroites," looked bright indeed. Dark clouds were gathering, however, in a locale far from the industrial heartland of Canada. In his home province of Saskatchewan, John George Diefenbaker was not just the newly elected Leader of Her Majesty's Opposition; the head of the Progressive Conservative party was also the messianic champion of the West and the downtrodden. He was poised to become the new prime minister of Canada in 1956.

Chapter 8
Flying the Arrow

On March 25, 1958, the Avro Aircraft Limited plant in Malton hummed with activity. That Tuesday morning, employees at Canada's largest aircraft manufacturer were hard at work, preparing the first Avro Arrow for its initial flight. The second shift of office staff had arrived, and even though most workers went through the motions, there was an expectant air about the plant. Kay Shaw, one of the engineers, overheard fellow staff members talking about the imminent maiden flight of the Arrow. Rumours had circulated around both Avro and its nearby subsidiary, Avro Orenda Engines, that the new bird would fly that day. One of the only Avro employees who knew for sure was "Shorty" Hatton, the company's chief experimental and test flight inspector. He would sign the all-important "Cleared for Flight" documents when both mechanical checks and the test pilot's recommendation came through.

One other Avro employee would clear the Avro Arrow for flight testing, and that was the chief development test pilot, Jan Zurakowski. As the pilot assigned to fly the aircraft, he had the last call as to whether it was ready to fly. Zura had lived with the CF-105 Arrow for years, shepherding it through its early development and helping to create the design of the sleek and powerful delta-wing interceptor. Tuesday morning was cool and hazy, not ideal flying weather, but if the forecasts held out, Zurakowski would fly.

In their cosy Toronto apartment, Anna, Janusz's wife, had been busy getting the two young Zurakowski boys to school when she'd had a premonition that this would be the day. While George was finishing his breakfast and Mark put on his boots, Anna cast a furtive look at her husband. He was his usual cheerful self, but there was a quickening of pace in his gathering of files that confirmed her hunch. Janusz never confided in his wife on occasions such as this.

A first test flight was fraught with danger. Would the aircraft hold together? Was it safe to fly? In a similar situation at his last company, Gloster Aircraft Company in England, Chief Test Pilot Bill Waterton had flown the prototype Javelin fighter on a test flight where everything had gone wrong. A piece of the tail had broken loose in flight and the wildly gyrating fighter had careened through the sky before Waterton managed to crash-land back at the base. He had been lucky; many others had not come back from an in-flight disaster like this.

Zurakowski kissed his wife goodbye and set out for the factory. By the time he arrived, the ground crew assigned to the experimental section had been going over the aircraft for hours. They had begun their day at six in the morning. Every main component and system had been checked, and when Zura did his "white glove" treatment they were sure he would find nothing wrong. The previous test flight had been cancelled three days earlier when he'd detected a hydraulic leak.

Zura had been known to go over an aircraft so thoroughly that he would find missing screws and point out the empty holes to offending mechanics and fitters. Worse still was Zura's return flight to the base. If he scooted by upside down, that was the signal that there were loose parts in the cockpit. He would fly upside down deliberately to pick up the parts that flew by him and landed on the cockpit. In his customary manner, he never chewed out any of the ground crew, but would insist that the aircraft be serviced properly. No crew member ever wanted to be the cause of Zurakowski's displeasure. They loved him that much.

By nine o'clock, Zura had done his walk-around and settled into the cockpit. Ray Hopper, the line chief, peered over his shoulder as seat belts were adjusted and all the oxygen lines and radio plugs were connected. Carefully, Zura went through the entire takeoff checklist. When he was ready, he signalled to Doc Staly and Johnnie Straboe to ground-start the Pratt and Whitney J-75 engines. These interim turbojets were installed while the definitive Orenda Iroquois engines were completing final tests. With a shriek, the sound of the jet engines tore through the airport.

John L. Plant, president and general manager at Avro Aircraft, heard the roar of the Avro Arrow. He went on the P.A. to announce that all non-essential employees, if they wished, could leave their tasks and see the test flight. With that, all the typewriters and machines at the plant seemed to stop at the same time, and more than 7000 employees streamed out of the factory. Word soon spread to the Orenda plant next door, and thousands more from that factory joined the throngs that appeared like magic outside the Avro hangars.

Two Avro chase planes were overhead. Spud Potocki flew a CF-100 with Hugh Mackechnie manning both still and cine cameras in the back seat, while F/L Jack Woodman was in a Canadair Sabre. He would record the flight using a movie camera mounted on top of his helmet.

At the run-up area, the Avro Arrow throbbed away, and then suddenly, with the release of brakes, the aircraft began to roll. Zurakowski read off the numbers as the Arrow approached takeoff velocity. At the one-third mark on Runway 32, he eased the control stick back. For an instant, the nose gear left the runway and gracefully the Avro Arrow left its earthly confines and took to the sky for the first time. Fred Lake in the company tower announced "Avro 201 off at 9:51 and cleared to company tower."

Climbing steadily on a northerly course at an initial

rate of climb of 3000 fpm at 200 knots, Zurakowski cautiously tested the plane's controls. Satisfied with the response from his gentle manoeuvres, he toggled the undercarriage switch, retracting the gear. A red warning light blinked on. It indicated the nose gear had not locked in place. The chase planes closed in and confirmed the retraction was normal. Zura noted the snag; it was merely a balky light switch. Continuing the 30-minute orientation flight with the chase planes hugging the Arrow, he wheeled back over the Avro factory for several formation passes. Ray Boone from Procurement saw "grown men and women wiping away the tears. Over the years these dedicated men and women gave blood, sweat, and tears as their contribution to that day. And now, it really happened, our beloved bird was in the air."

Bill Gunston, a correspondent for *Flight* magazine, who had camped out near the runway, marvelled at the power and majesty of the aircraft as Zurakowski lined up for a straight-in approach. He flared dramatically at 160 knots, touching down in a slight puff of tire smoke when the brakes bit hard, streaming the bright red and white drag chute.

As he coasted to a stop in the run-up area, Zurakowski and the Arrow were greeted by a throng of Avro employees and well-wishers. Hoisted on the shoulders of the flight test engineers and flight crew, he was carried to the factory as the all-conquering hero.

The flight had been a vindication of sorts for Zurakowski. During the computer simulator training conducted by Stan

Arrow RL-201 on its first flight, circling the Avro Aircraft plant.

Kwiatkowski, Avro's resident computer expert, the mighty IBM 704 had defeated the best efforts of all the test pilots. The simulator runs returned alarming results. Potocki had only lasted seconds at the controls before crashing, and when the Great Zura took his turn, it was even worse. Kwiatkowski called in IBM, but the U.S. specialists were convinced the computer was right, and that the Avro Arrow would be a disaster. Zura scoffed at the notion. He told Floyd to get the airplane ready and that he would fly it. He was right — the

Arrow flew beautifully from the first flight to the last.

On the maiden flight, Zurakowski had noted two errors: the faulty warning light and a balky air conditioner control. The snag sheet was pinned to the wall in the Flight Test Office like a trophy.

For the next round of evaluation tests, Zurakowski took the lead in flying each of the Avro Arrows as they rolled off the assembly line. Other test pilots began to join him, Spud Potocki eventually putting more time at the controls than any other pilot. Peter Cope followed Potocki, while Jack Woodman, as an RCAF acceptance pilot, was checked out on the air force's future fighter. As 1958 drew to a close, other Avro and RCAF test pilots prepared for their first flights.

Although the test program was largely flawless, there were some instances of breakdowns that could have derailed the tests. The undercarriage was always a source of concern at Avro. Dowty had taken pride in designing a complex but delicate system that had to perform a series of actions in the retraction and stowage of the main gear. Zurakowski had once remarked to an official at Dowty that he much preferred a simpler and more robust gear. On the eleventh flight, his concerns about the undercarriage were dramatically underscored when the right landing gear came down but did not make the complete cycle to lock in place properly.

Zurakowski landed normally, but, without warning, the airplane skidded wildly to the right. Thinking that his drag chute had fouled, he released it. The Arrow continued off the runway and into the grass. With a sickening crack, the right gear leg snapped off and the airplane ground to a halt. It was merely a slipping chain on the rotating gear, but when the repairs were carried out at Dowty, a stronger and less complicated Mk.2 undercarriage was fitted. Zura had been right again.

Potocki would also sheer off an undercarriage leg in landing, but this time it wasn't the landing gear that was to blame. The Arrow was the first aircraft to employ a fly-by-wire system where electric pulses were used to connect the pilot inputs to control surfaces. Flying RL-202, Potocki had landed, but heavy braking blew out all four main tires. The left main gear leg broke in two as the Arrow ran off the runway. The air force labelled the "prang," or crash, a pilot error. Zurakowski, however, protested that Potocki would never cause an accident. Two high-school kids who had snuck inside the factory perimeter would ultimately prove Zurakowski had had reason to doubt the initial findings. When the boys' camera was confiscated, Avro employees realized that they had photographed the Potocki accident. One of the photos revealed that the elevators were locked fully down, producing a heavy load on the wing, which backed up what Zurakowski found in the telemetry data for the flight.

The flight control system had momentarily reversed itself and had planted the Arrow down on the ground harder than the pilot had wished. Braking had caused the highly stressed tires to blow. The Dunlop tires were inflated to

200 psi, and when they exploded like they had countless times during Zurakowski's taxi tests, they blew off the gear like shrapnel. Zura eventually solved the tire blowout problems, but the Arrow's fly-by-wire system that had troubled Potocki would nearly kill Zurakowski on a later flight.

The first test of the automatic flight control system began with a normal takeoff. Just off the runway, with the landing gear folding away, Zurakowski flicked a switch on his control stick to go into an automatic mode in which the aircraft would take over. Immediately, the giant craft flicked into a roll, heading straight for the concrete below. Without a moment's hesitation, Zurakowski flipped the switch off with his thumb and regained control, scant feet from the ground. When he repeated the test at a safe altitude, the Arrow twisted violently into a roll again and was only restored to normal flight when the automatic controls were shut off. Technicians traced the problem to a faulty circuit. To Zurakowski, none of these problems was serious. He was proved accurate in his assessment; the Avro Arrow proceeded rapidly through the first stage of airworthiness and performance trials, even though the Iroquois engines were not yet installed.

While flying RL-204 on February 2, 1959, test pilot Peter Cope witnessed an unusual sight. Lying on its belly across the intersection of the two main runways at Malton was a Trans-Canada Airlines Viscount. Running low on fuel, Cope radioed in to the Avro control tower for instructions. He was informed that the Viscount had landed wheels-up and could not be immediately removed. His flight plan was altered to divert to RCAF Station Trenton, 58 kilometres away. Landing the Arrow at Trenton posed no great problems until Cope rolled to a stop and shut down. He cracked open the clamshell canopies and peered out — and down. The Arrow cockpit sat majestically more than 12 feet above the runway. Now what? Back at Malton, a special boarding ladder was used for ascent or descent from either of the two cockpits. As gracefully as he could, Cope scrambled over the side and down the leading edge of the wing until he was at a point where he could drop to the runway. Once on the ground, he and the Arrow were a big hit with the assembled RCAF pilots and ground crew. The next morning, the Avro "hack" DC-3 flew in with ground support equipment (including a boarding ladder) so that the Arrow engines could be fired up and Spud Potocki, who was to fly it back home to Malton, could get back into the cockpit.

The majority of the test flights were monitored by the RCAF radar tracking station in Edgar, Ontario, which was part of the NORAD (North American air defences) chain. On Zura's seventh flight, he dashed from Georgian Bay to Kingston, Ontario, directly over RCAF Edgar. Engineer Fred Matthews monitored flight communications back at Operations, and picked up the excited RCAF radar operator, "Look at that son-of-a-bitch go! Will you look at that son-of-a-bitch go!" Zurakowski hit Mach 1.52 (1157 mph) on RL-201 during that flight.

Even without the lighter and more powerful Iroquois engines, the Avro Arrow was proving to be the fastest thing in the sky. Tests showed that the Arrow had achieved Mach 1.98 at over 50,000 feet. The 18 months of testing now culminated in the Avro Arrow being prepared for an exciting event. Flight Test Operations began plans to set the world's speed and altitude records with RL-206, the first Iroquois-powered version, scheduled to fly in late February 1959.

Chapter 9
"Black Friday"

In 1957, even as the company was celebrating the rollout of the first Arrow, C.D. Howe had begun to have serious reservations about the viability of the program. In the House of Commons he said the massive outlay of funds had "given him the shudders."

If the greatest champion of A.V. Roe Canada had doubts, the fiery leader of the Opposition had no qualms about his views concerning Howe and his projects. Progressive Conservative leader John Diefenbaker had earned his reputation as a tough customer both in the courtroom and in the rough-and-tumble of the House of Commons. He set his sights squarely on the divisive Trans-Canada Pipeline debate and coined the damning "what's a million?" remark to describe Howe's cavalier treatment of the issue. Howe had been the flashpoint of Opposition anger throughout the contentious pipeline debate. He had always thought in grand schemes, although he was very much aware of the great expenditures that had already fuelled his "prize" projects, including the Avro Arrow. While Howe was dismissive of many of the Opposition arguments, his use of "closure' to end the Commons deliberations was remarkably ill-considered. John Diefenbaker seized the opportunity, declaring Howe was running roughshod over the House of Commons.

Using the debate as a cornerstone of his election platform, Diefenbaker scored a surprising victory over the long-standing Liberal government in 1957. As a crowning achievement, Diefenbaker crowed over the defeat of C.D. Howe in his home riding, albeit to a member of the CCF (Co-operative Commonwealth Federation, the forerunner of the New Democratic Party).

The first danger signs from the newly elected Diefenbaker government came late in 1957, when an internal review by George R. Pearkes, the new Minister of Defence, hinged on the impact of an escalating Soviet missile threat, brought to the forefront by the successes of the Sputnik and the Soviet space program. Largely heeding the direction that the U.S. and Great Britain had taken concerning the manned interceptor aircraft role, Pearkes had re-evaluated his position on the Avro Arrow's mission in the months following his public declarations at the Arrow rollout ceremony. At this juncture, Pearkes had consulted with the chiefs of staff and received some conflicting messages. While the RCAF's Air Marshal Hugh L. Campbell had vehemently protested, the other chiefs of staff had argued that the Arrow would drain funds from any other armed forces program. The recommendation had left the decision up to Pearkes.

Major General Pearkes, VC, had had a lengthy career in the army. He had received the Victoria Cross for heroic action at Passchendaele in 1917 and had served honourably in the Second World War. After entering politics, he had gravitated first to the post of defence critic and then was elevated to the position of Minister of Defence in 1957. Described unfavourably by some political observers as a "Colonel Blimp" figure straight out of the turn-of-the-century British Empire, Pearkes' first months in office had not been easy.

Though relying heavily on advice from military experts, Pearkes was also seeking advice elsewhere. Signing the NORAD agreement early in his tenure had created an integrated RCAF/USAF organization for continental air defence. The U.S., which had recently supplemented its ring of defence bases with guided missiles, was shopping the Boeing IM-99 Bomarc around. American military and industry representatives were aggressively promoting this point-defence missile to Canada as an effective alternative to the manned interceptor. The problematic Bomarc had garnered a reputation for test failures and a lack of accuracy in intercepting targets. A desperate effort to save the program depended on Canada's involvement in the "picket line" of Bomarc bases stretching across the northern border states.

Early in 1958, Pearkes and his ministerial officials made a half-hearted effort to interest the Americans in purchasing the Avro Arrow. Pearkes came away from his U.S. visit with a sale. He had bought the Bomarc.

Cost-effectiveness in buying an "off-the-shelf" weapon had been the telling factor for Pearkes. When the U.S. sweetened the deal by providing financial assistance in building missile bases, the Canadian government signed on the dotted line. However, when something looks too good to be true, it is. Perhaps Pearkes was aware that the nuclear warhead the Bomarc packed was essential to its lethal punch. Some observers rationalized that the small nuclear explosion that was triggered was the only way a Bomarc would be able to bring down an intruder, since it was fundamentally inaccurate. But if Pearkes knew he was buying a nuclear arsenal, Diefenbaker certainly did not. He had campaigned on Canada remaining a non-nuclear proliferating nation.

Crawford Gordon recognized the warning signs that the government was leaning towards outright cancellation of the Avro Arrow. He put up a brave front at the head office, but the pressures of the job were getting to him. At the very time when he should have provided leadership, his world was collapsing around him. He had just left his wife and family and was drinking heavily. The day-to-day work at the head office was taken over by the stalwart Fred Smye, who could not keep up the pretence that everything was normal.

Even though Smye had set up a meeting with the prime minister, the bull-headed Gordon wasn't listening anymore. Kept stewing in the antechamber, Gordon worked up a liquor-fuelled rage against the man who was threatening to destroy the Arrow and his company. He stormed into Diefenbaker's office, demanding that the Arrow continue. Slamming his fist on the prime minister's desk, he screamed out his demands. Whatever could be said about John Diefenbaker, he was not a coward and certainly would not back down in the face of a swaggering bully. To top it off, Dief was a tee-totaller; he abhorred the lushes who worked the cocktail circuits. The acrimonious row ended with Diefenbaker showing Gordon the door. That meeting put an end to any hope that the Arrow would survive. The sordid incident had been observed by Grattan O'Leary, Diefenbaker's "bag-man." He hadn't recognized Crawford Gordon, but he recalled that the figure departing the PM's office was "white as a sheet." Dief dismissed the whole affair with the words, "I have just told him that the thing is off."

Three days later, on September 23, 1958, John Diefenbaker made a public statement that the Avro Arrow program and its related Orenda Iroquois engines were being reviewed. The costly and problematic fire-control system and missile armament were cancelled, but no outright program cancellation was being announced. As an aside, Diefenbaker also reported that the Bomarc guided missile had been purchased. Reporters read into the statement that the Arrow's time had come. At Avro, an impossibly Pollyanna outlook took hold. Upon learning that a final review was delayed until March 1959, Gordon and senior management, grasping at straws, began planning a last-ditch media campaign to bolster the image of the Avro Arrow. Smye warned Gordon that the tough old birds of the Toronto press wouldn't look favourably on any ham-handed efforts at this late stage. He was right — the media crucified the Arrow.

The public perception of the Arrow in 1958 was decidedly mixed. To the people in the industrial heartland of Ontario, where aerospace and aviation industries were vital components of the economy, any threats to their well being were felt acutely. To the rest of the country, if opinions could be judged by newspaper headlines or letters to the editors, there was very little support for an expensive and risky high-tech project like the Avro Arrow. Gordon's intense media blitz failed miserably and only served to antagonize the government further. Diefenbaker took this Avro campaign as an open challenge, raging to sympathetic reporters that he would not be bullied. Cabinet documents from the period reveal that the prime minister vacillated in setting the deadline for outright cancellation, but never wavered from his resolve to put an end to the Avro Arrow. Quietly, orders went out to RCAF officials to wind up the Arrow project office.

By this time, Janusz Zurakowski was 44, old for a test pilot. He had made a promise to his wife that he would retire at 40, and only the Avro Arrow had enticed him to stay past that date. When the bulk of the test program was completed, and the other test pilots had checked out on the Arrow, Zura announced his retirement from test flying. He would become a liaison engineer in the Flight Test office, still involved with the acceptance trials of the Avro Arrow. Zurakowski was convinced that the results of the testing would show that the Arrow was unquestionably the finest interceptor aircraft in the world. His last assignment was coordinating a test flight on February 19 in which Spud Potocki flew RL-203 with a flight observer aboard. It was the only time an Arrow carried a passenger. It would also be the last flight of an Avro Arrow.

Jan Zurakowski was at his desk on February 20 when the call came in at 9:15 a.m. The breathless voice on the phone was a *Toronto Telegram* reporter who blurted out, "Have you heard? Dief's done it. He's cancelled the Arrow." Zurakowski couldn't believe the report. He quickly wheeled out of his chair and buttonholed one of the executives in the Administration Building. He saw the shock in the man's face. No one knew anything. Besides, the decision wasn't coming down that day, said John Plant, the president at Avro Aircraft. The government had promised to make the report final in March. The silence in the main office was abruptly broken by the clattering of the teletype machine set up in the corner of the room.

Ron A. Williams, Crawford Gordon's assistant, peeled off the printout. It was true; the official notice of cancellation had arrived. Avro executives retreated to the boardroom to decide their next course of action. The government order was clear. It stated, in part, "Formal notice of termination is being given now to the contractor." Plant felt that everyone had to be let go. He checked once more with the legal department, who confirmed that the rigid provisions of the contracts for trades people as well as technical staff left no option. At 11:15 a.m., Plant's voice rang out over the factory's public address system.

Everyone there that day remembered the sombre tones of the "Black Friday" message, but couldn't recall the exact words. Plant had formally announced the end of the Avro Arrow program and its accompanying Iroquois engines by merely stating that the Arrow was being cancelled and that all employees had to quit work and make arrangements to leave the factory. Regardless of the words used, it was clear to the morning shift: it was all over.

High above the Avro plant, Stan Haswell was completing a test of the second-to-last production CF-100 fighter. He checked in with the company tower for instructions only to be told to come in; there was no need to continue the test. A similar message was relayed to Mike Cooper-Slipper who was also in the air, conducting a test of the Orenda Iroquois engine mounted on the B-47 test bed. It would be the last time the Iroquois would be fired up. The first lines of employees were now snaking out of the buildings into the teeth of a fierce blizzard and an uncertain future. Bill Beatty of CBC Radio, who was already stationed at the parking lot gates, said he was witnessing "a funeral procession of hundreds of cars, lined up bumper-to-bumper, carrying toolmakers, engineers and office workers from the plant for the last time."

By the weekend, the gigantic facilities at the aircraft and engine divisions were empty. The five completed Arrows sat forlornly outside the flight test hangar. Inside the factory, the partially assembled fleet of fighters was abandoned in Assembly Bay 3. February 23, 1959, marked the 50th anniversary of the first powered flight in Canada. All official celebrations pointedly left out references to the Avro Arrow and the commemorative stamp issued by the Post Office.

A skeleton crew of maintenance and security staff were recalled from the massive list of layoffs. For the next weeks, they roamed the plants, furtively casting a glance at each other and wondering how long they would retain even these jobs. In April 1959, another crew moved into the Avro plant.

A squad of armed forces personnel swept through the offices of the Avro Company, collecting all records of the CF-105 Arrow including blueprints, photographs, models, and films. They were operating under a sweeping directive to destroy all sensitive material pertaining to the project. When questioned in the House, the Minister of Defence initially was unaware of the events at the Avro plant. Only much later was it revealed that Crown Assets, the government department tasked with the closing down of the Avro Arrow, justified the destruction as triggered by the government decision to end the project. When Lou Wise, head of the Photographic

Department, was ordered to destroy all of the Arrow material, on his own volition he carefully prepared copies of everything and publicly destroyed only the copies. The day after the destruct order was in effect, Wise called in a bevy of military people to watch his incineration of photographic stock, film, and files. The bonfire in his office made a pretty picture but secretly, he had ensured that original material was safe. He hid a pristine 16 mm film, *Supersonic Sentinel,* in his home.

The same thing was happening everywhere: some workers stuffed blueprints into lunch boxes and walked out of the factory, right under the noses of the security staff. Small caches of tools, parts, and other Arrow memorabilia survived through the ingenuity of ordinary Avro employees. The efforts of one government official also led to the rescue of countless remnants of the Avro Arrow and Iroquois engines. Mac Kuhring, head of the National Research Council Engine Laboratory, requested an exhaustive list of materials that would serve to document the evolution of technology in the Avro and Orenda programs. Pallets of equipment, tooling, assemblies and manuals all marked "classified" were accepted en masse and secreted away in the NRC facilities at Ottawa. At the far-away Nobel test facility, John Armstrong, the engineer-in-charge, half-heartedly carried out the Crown Assets orders to mothball the plant. Many components of the Avro Iroquois engine that were being tested survived at Nobel, as well as at Orenda, where Chief Engineer Ian Ferrar made sure that at least two complete engines were secured in the Rheem container area behind the plant.

Fred Smye was astonished to find that the military's orders extended to the destruction of the completed Arrows, as well as all the aircraft still on the production line. At first, he refused to obey the order, but the pressure from the government, laden with implied repercussions for the company, was relentless. To his everlasting regret, he acquiesced. In the end, the threat of army intervention in the plant forced Smye to let the demolition begin. Lou McPherson was part of a team of Avro technicians who began removing components from the group of test aircraft. He used an arc welder to cut the nose cone off RL-201. "It just broke me up to do it. I hated the idea of cutting up this dream we all had. But we had to do it." Another group of workers was sent to begin dismantling the production line.

Jim Floyd protested vehemently, showing Smye requests from both the USAF and RAF for the remaining Arrows. The British test establishment at Boscombe Down sent a proposal to take three completed Arrows along with spares as part of a supersonic project. Floyd had proceeded to plan the logistical support for a transatlantic flight just days before the destruction orders came into effect. On his own initiative, Smye had also canvassed an assistant secretary of the USAF and obtained a verbal commitment for assistance to keep the Arrow production lines at Avro going. The U.S. support included the supply of radar, fire-control systems, and missiles, along with unrestricted use of the flight test centre at Muroc, California. These donations would have considerably reduced the development costs of the Avro Arrow. Smye immediately contacted the defence production deputy minister's office with the news and waited expectantly for a reply. He would wait in vain. Later, on record, the deputy minister commented derisively that, as a weapons system, "there never was an Arrow."

Orders had come down from Sir Roy Dobson himself to salvage whatever could be saved of the company's future. But, as the only executive with any authority left, Gordon having retreated in a drunken haze to the company's posh Briarcrest sanctuary and Plant already gone, Smye could do nothing to stop the destruction. Worse was to come.

The Lax Brothers Scrapyard in Hamilton purchased the remains of the Arrow project from Crown Assets after bidding $300,000 for the lot — airplanes, jigs and tools, and any related fixtures. The work was done rapidly behind closed doors. Due to their unfamiliarity with aircraft, the salvage crew had brought a wrecking ball that clanged off a hardened section of a fuselage, bouncing straight back and nearly hitting the operator. Blowtorches were no better as the exotic materials found in the aircraft, such as magnesium and titanium, would prove lethal if ignited. The workers settled on axes and saws to crudely dismember the airframes. The jigs and tooling inside the plant were cut apart with acetylene torches.

Even though no Avro employee could get close to the

The Avro Arrows being cut up.

salvage operation, Elwy Yost clearly remembered the scene: "I'll never forget one thing, the smell of acetylene torches that were being used ...." He also noticed that the few Avroites left in the building were crying. It was a heartbreaking end to the dream of the Avro Arrow.

Left dormant on the drawing boards was the follow-up series of Arrows. The Arrow 2A would have had a much greater range due to increased fuel storage. The Mark 3 would be a more radical development capable of Mach 3+ "dash" performance at over 70,000 feet altitude. This version would have featured variable geometry intakes and the use of heat-resistant materials in sensitive areas of the airframe and engines. Other Arrows included reconnaissance, bomber, and trainer variants. A unique Zero-length launch system was also proposed where a combination of booster rockets and an angled ramp set at a 20-degree angle would be able to catapult an Arrow into flight. The most advanced derivatives, tentatively known as the Mark 4 series, would feature the capability of an anti-ICBM (Intercontinental Ballistic Missile) launch platform that would intercept nuclear-tipped missiles at the edge of space.

The likely prospects of sales of the Orenda Iroquois were also dashed. Both Dassault Aviation in France (in negotiations to purchase 300 engines for their Mirage IV bomber) and Curtiss-Wright in the U.S. had entered into an agreement for license manufacture. They were told that all deals were off. One last desperate solution to save the Iroquois program revolved around the possible selection of the Republic F-105, equipped with the Orenda Iroquois, as Canada's new tactical fighter for the NATO "strike fighter" role. Both Republic Aircraft and Avro presented a joint submission to the Canadian government in the days following the Arrow's cancellation. Fred Smye noted in his memoirs that the executives went to Ottawa to make a detailed case, but with the prevailing mood of the government, he recorded sadly, "that was the last that was heard of that."

An intriguing mystery remains concerning the midnight theft of RL-206, the first Avro Arrow Mk.2's cockpit and nose section. Dr. John Young from the Aerospace Medical Centre at RCAF Downsview engineered the audacious plot. Commandeering a flat bed trailer, a small crew loaded and transported the Arrow parts across town to a site specially prepared in the centre. Once the parts were stored in the corner room, it was sealed off with a concrete block that was painted to match the surrounding walls. The last remains of the Arrow were kept hidden until late in the 1960s, when they appeared mysteriously in the storage compound of RCAF Trenton. Or at least that's how the story goes. Like much of the Avro Arrow lore, there is a hint of truth wrapped up in an enigma.

The cockpit of the first Mk.2 Arrow actually served as high-altitude chamber for a number of years at the Institute for Aviation Medicine at RCAF Downsview, where RCAF pilots were subjected to simulated conditions up to 50,000 feet altitude in a low-pressure environment. Upon its belated discovery in RCAF storage, RL-206 was then transferred to the aeronautical collection of the National Museum of Science and Technology in Ottawa. Today, the sole remnants of the Arrow are on display in the Canada Aviation Museum in Rockliffe, Ontario.

Chapter 10
Desperate Times

Within moments of the Avro Arrow's cancellation, all the employees of the once-great company were unemployed. Most of the nearly 15,000 employees of the Avro and Orenda factories would never come back. Many of them wouldn't find a job in aviation again. The ripple effect of layoffs extended to the 600 sub-contractors in the Avro parts and supply chain. As far away as Bristol Aerospace in Winnipeg, where the Arrow tail cone was produced, six workers were released. An estimated 30,000 employees lost their jobs due to the Avro Arrow's cancellation. For the fliers who had harnessed the power of the Arrow to launch the interceptor into the stratosphere, the more crucial choices they had to make was where their next paycheque would come from or whether they would ever fly again. Four of them never would.

Sir Roy Dobson flew to Canada to take personal control of the crisis in his empire. He met with Diefenbaker to get an assessment of the situation. Dobson came away from the meeting with a sinking feeling that he had to gut the executives who had mishandled the debacle. The parent company, A.V. Roe Canada, still controlled vast divisions that manufactured ships, rail cars, buses, and railway stock, as well as being heavily committed to coal, iron, and steel production. All of these programs depended heavily on Canadian government contracts.

Even though he had treated Crawford Gordon like a son, Dobson realized Gordon would have to be one of the first "Mahogany Row" executives to go. Sir Roy demanded his resignation, hoping that this act would mollify the government. It didn't. Despite Smye's hope that Avro's submissions for new aircraft projects would provide a temporary reprieve for the company, the Diefenbaker government, upset by the public furore over the layoffs, refused to deal with Avro. Pearkes offered the bizarre suggestion to Fred Smye that the company simply had to re-tool to produce new products. He suggested automobiles. Smye couldn't believe his ears; the enormity of converting the factory operation would mean abandoning any hope of producing aircraft again.

Recruiters from prominent aerospace companies flocked to Toronto to snag the cream of the Avro technical and engineering staff. The most brazen headhunters set up shop in Avro's parking lots, inviting scores of Avroites to pack up and come to the United Kingdom and the United States. Most recruitment took place at the North York Hotel in downtown Toronto, where representatives from Lockheed, Boeing, North American Rockwell, and Bell were headquartered. Jim Floyd made a pledge to his engineering staff that he would find them alternative jobs. He was true to his word. Floyd, along with a select group of Avro engineers, went back home to England to work for Hawker-Siddeley on an advanced supersonic transport, leading to the Concorde.

One of the greatest coups for recruiters was in hiring Jim Chamberlin and 25 Avro Arrow engineers for the fledgling National Aeronautics and Space Administration (NASA). Chamberlin headed up the engineering department on the Mercury and Gemini Projects before developing the lunar orbit mission of Project Apollo. All of the former Avro engineers made important contributions to NASA: R. Bryan Erb helped develop the Apollo heat shield; Owen Maynard became chief of the Systems Engineering Division at Apollo; John Hodge, Frederick Matthews, and Tex Roberts ran Mission Control; Rodney Rose was in Mission Planning, along with Peter Armitage, who was involved in the recovery systems for Mercury, Gemini, and Apollo missions. Known as the "Avro group," the influence of this large engineering group from Avro has been compared to that of Werner von Braun's initial team of German rocket scientists recruited just after the end of World War Two.

More than just the employees were affected by the layoffs. The Avro Aircraft and Orenda companies dominated the lives of the village of Malton and surrounding communities. Over 90 percent of the tax assessment of Malton came from the Avro and Orenda facilities. The plants had supplied water to both Malton and the airport that Avro shared with the city of Toronto. The relationship was so close that Avro Auxiliary volunteers carried out most of the municipal policing and when a fire broke out at the airport, the Avro fire department was called in.

The sense of betrayal felt by scores of embittered Avroites led them to simply walk away from their homes and begin new lives elsewhere in Canada. Others left the country for good. Numerous breakups occurred in Avro families. George Foley's father lost his job as a tool-and-die maker; he never worked in the aviation industry again. The Foley family eventually fractured and scattered throughout Ontario and Western Canada. More ominously, countless suicides would also be attributed to Black Friday.

Nevertheless, following the cancellation of the Arrow and Iroquois engine projects, small maintenance contracts for the CF-100 and Orenda engines still in service would result in 1500 technical staff being called back.

A reappraisal of the research and development currently on the go at Avro was discouraging. None of the work would generate new projects. The Avro Project Research Group would, however, provide tantalizing hints of future concepts with investigations into purely theoretical research, as well as the evaluation of projects for both military and civil applications. It has been estimated that over 70 percent of all industrial research and development in Canada throughout the 1950s had been carried out by A.V. Roe Canada. All of the projects were cancelled in the wake of Black Friday.

More practical efforts by Mario Pesando had centred on aviation and missile programs, which led to Avro proposals for a ship-borne missile to meet a Royal Canadian Navy requirement and an anti-tank missile to be used by Canadian Army infantry. A vertical-takeoff–and-landing (VTOL) version of the CF-100 using Bristol Orpheus lift-jets, as well as a new supersonic V/STOL (vertical or short takeoff) fighter design, were submissions to meet NATO specifications for a tactical fighter. In an attempt to re-enter the civil aircraft field, Jim Floyd's Design Office continued to come up with new designs, including a mid-size four-engined jet transport, a small business jet tailored around two rear-mounted jets, and even studies into a supersonic airliner.

An advanced transportation projects group led by Rolf Marshall had developed a giant 200-ton capacity "Big-Wheel Transport" for arctic travel that did not proceed further than a sales brochure. More promising was the turbine-powered Mono-Rail rapid transit system designed for use in Toronto. The "Tractor" turbine-powered transport and "Bobcat" all-terrain tracked armoured personnel carrier were built as prototypes and demonstrated to military and commercial clients.

Most intriguing yet was the pure research into nuclear and chemical power plants, automation, electronics, and advanced composite materials. Designs by James Chamberlin for a hypersonic (Mach 5) vehicle led to an advanced STV (Space Threshold Vehicle) that closely approximated the Space Shuttle concept. One other project was underway in the secretive Special Projects Group run by John Frost. Since 1954, U.S. military backing had sustained a remarkable "flying saucer" research and development effort. The first prototypes of the Avro VZ-9-AV Avrocar were about to come off the tiny production line set up in the Experimental Flight Test Hangar. In desperation, Avro would try to pump as many staff as they could into this project, swelling the Avrocar team into the hundreds.

Frost's research had focused on an advanced supersonic disk-shaped fighter, built in full-scale form in the Shaeffer Building. The Avrocar, however, would be a tiny "proof-of-concept" test vehicle that would only demonstrate hovering and low-speed performance. The USAF and U.S. Army were the sole funding agencies for the project. Pursuing army interest in hovering capability, Frost also designed a series of "Avromobiles" and "Avroskimmers," which remained paper projects. In 1959, the U.S. Design Office, in light of the chaos at Avro Canada, halted the entire program. Frost, ever the consummate salesman, convinced the Americans to restart the project. He was acutely aware that the Avrocar was a gigantic gamble for Avro, knowing the first ground tests had shown that the test vehicle would barely be able to get off the ground. Dobson and senior management would not fund any further development.

There were only a few test pilots left in Don Rogers group. Zurakowski was long gone. Spud Potocki became the senior pilot on the Avrocar with Peter Cope as backup. After five months of engine testing, the first model was shipped to the NASA Ames wind tunnel in California, while the second Avrocar was prepared for its maiden flight.

On December 5, 1959, Spud Potocki, bedecked in a specially made asbestos flight suit, approached the Avrocar warily. There was no provision for an ejection seat and only his recent practice in scrambling out of the pilot's cockpit assured him that an escape would be possible. For the last test hops, three restraining cables had held the vehicle down, but he had struggled with the controls. This was not like any other aircraft he had ever flown. Compared to the Arrow, the dumpy little saucer did not even look the part. More work on the simulator had given him confidence that he could master the skittish devil.

Firing up the three J69 turbojets (which were housed perilously close to the two cockpits) produced a tremendous heat throughout the airframe. Instruments would be baked brown after only a few hours. At least cold weather would help keep the heat down. Pushing throttles to full power, Potocki felt the little craft wobble and then gradually rise. Tiny movements on the side-control stick pushed the Avrocar sideways then forward. Gaining some forward momentum, Spud drew the nose up cautiously to a metre above the ground, still safe in a cushion of air that cradled the craft.

After a few minutes of tentative manoeuvres, Potocki pushed the Avrocar into a sharper turn. Immediately, the nose pitched violently down. As he pulled back on the controls, the vehicle began to wobble, pitching forward, backward, and sideways faster than his control movements could catch the opposite action. Fearing an imminent crash, Potocki throttled back. The Avrocar spun like a tiddly-wink to the ground, landing on its miniature outrigger wheels with a thud. Frost's worse fears were confirmed: the Avrocar would remain nothing more than a hovercraft. Attempting to fly it out of ground cushion would generate the "hubcapping" effect that Potocki had discovered. Although an extensive flying program eventually solved most of its handling problems, the hapless Avrocar remained a marginal performer, barely able to reach highway speeds at a grand altitude of three feet.

With the failure of the Avrocar flying tests, the last of Avro's aviation programs ground to an inevitable halt as the U.S. funding ran out. The supersonic test model was broken up and the two Avrocars were retained by the U.S. military, eventually ending up in museums stateside.

In 1960, Dobson and the Hawker-Siddeley Group made one last effort to save Avro. Faced with the dilemma that the largest factory in the organization was virtually a "ghost town," a wide range of new production proposals was evaluated. Although joint ventures between Avro Aircraft and U.S. aircraft manufacturers did not receive support from the government, even embracing the idea proposed by George Pearkes, a proposal by American Motors to build Ramblers was considered, but like all the others, died in the planning stages. Earl Brownridge, executive vice president and general manager of Orenda Engines, and one of the few "Mahogany Row" executives left in the company, proposed a new car project. He loved sports cars and thought that a market existed for a high-performance two-seater. Using aircraft technology, the Design Office turned out a beautiful aluminum-bodied roadster. Brownridge got to sit in the completed prototype. That's as far as the project went.

Investing heavily in a radical departure from aviation, a production line of Richardson aluminium cruisers was set up as a trial venture. Working with the Richardson Boat Company, a new design based on aircraft materials and manufacturing techniques was produced, but after only a few dozen boats had been completed, the project was cancelled. Dobson realized that due to the complexity of the aluminium construction, the Richardson boats were too expensive to build and after only a small number of sales, it was also clear there was no market for a new luxury cruiser.

The final work in the nearly empty plants at Malton was manufacturing steel pots and pans, a humiliating end for Canada's once-booming aviation giant, the birthplace of the

Avro Jetliner, CF-100 fighter, and the Avro Arrow. Due to continual modifications and refinements, the CF-100 became one of the outstanding all-weather fighter interceptors of the 1950s and 1960s. The sturdy "Clunk" or "Lead Sled" soldiered on for over 30 years in Canadian and Belgian air forces. Its service life in the RCAF and CAF (Canadian Armed Forces) would eventually stretch into the 1980s as its role changed to electronic countermeasures. It was the only Avro product to go into production and operational service.

On one of his final trips to Canada, Sir Roy Dobson presided over the last rites of the company he had built. In looking around the A.V. Roe Canada boardroom, he sadly noted that he did not recognize anyone. On April 30, 1962, the company was renamed Hawker Siddeley Canada and its operations wound down. Orenda Engines continued manufacturing engines in a fraction of its original plant, before being absorbed in a buy-out later in the 1980s.

Chapter 11
Legend or Myth?

Each of the men and women coming through the security gates at the Boeing Administration Building clutched a formal invitation. Most of the older people brought something else with them. Some wore faded nametags; former engineer Desmond Todd recited his badge number to Laura Cooke, a present-day Boeing Toronto employee, who smiled and cheerily motioned him in. This would be the first time in a very long time that 300 former Avro employees had come back home.

The passing years had seen many changes at the Malton facility. De Havilland Canada had taken over the factory site, but had sold the property to McDonnell Douglas in 1967. For 30 years, DC-9 wings and individual components had been manufactured there, but when Boeing had taken over, there had been little need for two million square feet of production space. Although the massive assembly hangars were still there, only a few areas of the plants were still in use. Most of the administration area had been shut down, and plans had already been put in place to demolish some of the empty buildings. A dramatic reduction in the staff had also taken place, leaving only 400 employees, compared to the 6000-strong workforce at the height of DC-9 production contracts.

On October 4, 2002, Stephen J. Fisher, the president of Boeing Toronto Ltd., marked the 45th anniversary of the rollout of the Avro CF-105 Arrow with a reunion of former Avro employees. Now in their late seventies or early eighties, the Avroites had come from across Canada and the United States to once more stand in the spot where the Arrow had been manufactured. In its place was a full-scale replica Arrow cockpit and nose section from the Toronto Aerospace Museum, brought by Claude Sherwood, who had once worked on the real Arrow.

On the site where more than 15,000 employees and guests had once cheered the Arrow's birth, Avroites returned to mark its passing. There were a few younger people in the crowd, including Brian Willer, an Avro "baby" who lovingly set out an interpretive display based on his collection of Avro artefacts. Private conversations in the presentation area revolved around memories of people and good times, but inevitably came back to the Arrow and the debate that had emerged surrounding its demise.

There were no more knowledgeable authorities on the subject of Canada's most controversial aviation project than this assemblage. Some of the principals in the story were present. Jim Floyd, Wilf Farrance, Don Rogers, and Lou Wise all had a piece of the puzzle, but others, such as C.D. Howe, Sir Roy Dobson, Fred Smye, and Crawford Gordon, had passed on. Gordon may have drunk himself to death, but it was the Arrow that had inflicted the first wound. It was like that for all the others, too. George Pearkes and John Diefenbaker, who had been privy to the reasons the government chose to cancel the program, were also deceased. In a sad aftermath of the Arrow debate, both men's careers suffered tragically. Pearkes left the Cabinet after National Defence issues such as rearmament with nuclear weapons slipped from his control, while Dief never completely recovered the public's confidence in the wake of the controversy. His memoirs likened the Avro Arrow to a seminal event that triggered his slow slide from power. In his later years, he would never speak publicly about the Arrow.

In recent years, the saga of the Avro Arrow has taken on mythic proportions. A cottage industry has materialized with countless books, movies, and a stage play about the Arrow. A 1997 television mini-series, a joint production of Winnipeg's John Aaron Productions and Tapestry Films and The Film Works of Toronto, served to stir the most passionate debate on the controversial aspects of the Arrow saga. Dubbed a docu-drama, *The Arrow* starred Dan Akroyd as Crawford Gordon and featured international stars Christopher Plummer, Michael Ironside, Michael Moriarity, and Canadian television stars Sarah Botsford, Ron White, and Aidan Devine. The mini-series introduced many of the present generation to a fascinating mix of political intrigue, technological achievements, and factual accounts with a sensational Hollywood approach. Principal photography was shifted to locations in Winnipeg, where the Western Canada Aviation Museum played the stand-in for the Avro factory. In the recesses of a wartime-vintage hangar, a full-scale model Avro Arrow was constructed for the movie. Albertan Allan Jackson completed the cockpit and nose along with landing gear as a hobby before the production team took over the project. The finished movie prop not only looked realistic, but was also able to taxi on its own power. Along with a series of exacting large-scale flying models designed by Doug and Donnette Hyslip, the movie models faithfully recreated the test flights of the Avro Arrow.

Although Avroites lamented the treatment of real people and events, one of the genuine highlights of the film was the blending of archival footage with live-action. The film *Supersonic Sentinel* featured prominently. When the production team contacted Lou Wise for permission to use his copy, the young production assistant commented that she seemed to recognize that distinct voice narrating the film.

Lou chuckled, "Of course you do, that's me on the film." Lou had been the narrator on all the Avro company productions and reprised that role for the mini-series.

Even though historians dismissed the farcical aspects of the production, the film reignited a national angst. The mini-series once again triggered debate over the reasons for cancellation of the project, with strong advocates on both sides of the argument. Historians Jack Granastein and Desmond Morton pointed out that the Arrow was too costly, too high-tech, and unable to do the mission for which it was designed. Yet the Arrow's demise marked the end of Canada's military aerospace industry and the beginning of a reliance on U.S. and foreign products. For some sociological observers, the loss of the remarkable Avro team in future research and development was even more devastating. The many thousands of scientists and engineers who left Canada were lost for good.

Among those who designed, built, and flew the Avro Arrow, there was unanimous consent that their beloved aircraft would have achieved greatness. In the wake of media reports following the mini-series, a few historians challenged this notion, but the one man who knew its potential, Janusz Zurakowski, entered the fray with this comment: "It was far ahead of its time, and it showed that this country was in the forefront in aircraft technology world wide. There will never be another Arrow."

Even though the reasons for cancellation were debatable, there was almost universal revulsion for the decision to destroy the Arrow. David Mackechnie had seen his late father's photographs and knew even as a child that something terrible had happened at the plant. Even as officials were denying it, the Avro Arrows were being chopped apart. He called it, "a mocking epitaph to the work of the men and women who built her."

A group photograph would be the last formal event at the Boeing Toronto reunion. Outside the assembly bay, a full-size painting of the Avro Arrow on the concrete was a poignant reminder to the audience of a glorious day when the Arrow stood proudly in the sunlight. The passage of time had tempered the raw emotions of Black Friday, but it had not taken away its impact. Jim Floyd gazed wistfully at the Arrow painting, remarking, "Returning to this spot has awakened a lot of ghosts and memories."

Randall Whitcomb, who also attended the reunion, is a noted Canadian aviation artist. A former air force pilot who flew the CF-18 Hornet, Whitcomb does more than paint oils of the Arrow at its zenith. He devotes much of his time to a stack of Avro company documents on loan from his good friend, James C. Floyd, the Avro Arrow's "father figure."

The artist is part of a worldwide network of Avro enthusiasts who have maintained that the Arrow was "murdered" by outside forces. His passion for his subject is well-documented. He champions the cause of the Avro Arrow throughout Canada with the intensity of a true believer. In a recent address in Alberta, Whitcomb emphatically declared, "while established history and public figures have all claimed that the U.S. had nothing to do with it, I have the smoking gun that proves they did." Launching into a detailed thesis from his book, *Avro Aircraft and Cold War Aviation,* he outlines his case: documents he has uncovered show that the American military-industrial complex orchestrated the deed. Perhaps it is true. Not everyone is convinced, but the U.S. conspiracy argument persists to this day as part of the all-encompassing mythology of the Avro Arrow.

The one enduring element of the myth of the Avro Arrow is the tale of the "one that got away." The story was perpetuated in a *Maclean's* magazine article by reporter June Callwood that appeared shortly after the Arrow's cancellation. In it, she related her experiences flying aboard the B-47 fitted with the test Iroquois engine destined for the Avro Arrow. Callwood, like many others of the period, was enamoured with the Arrow; she wrote, "it was the most beautiful plane I will ever see ... When it lifted straight up into the sky, a slim white arrowhead, it was poetry. I never saw it take off without my eyes stinging ..." Since she had flown in the B-47/Orenda test bed, when she was startled awake one morning by the roar of an Arrow's engines filling the sky above her, she thought "someone had flown an Arrow to safety." Most Avroites knew the truth. None had escaped the wrath of the demolition crew's axes. But one Avro engineer had almost pulled it off.

The date was April 22, 1959. Gerry Barbour, an Avro Aircraft engineer in the Lofting Department, where blueprint drawings were scribed on metal sections before being cut out, was furious at the decision to cancel the Arrow, but was even more enraged by the scrapping of all the aircraft. As he watched foreman Al Cox begin the butchering of the five flying examples, Barbour formulated an elaborate heist. He had access to the high-security area, where he would steal a "mule" (a small tow truck) and tow one of the complete airframes to a horse-breeding farm he had in mind as a hiding place. His plans had gone as far as imagining his friend, Lorne Ursel, as the pilot of the aircraft. He settled on RL-204 as his target. This Arrow sat at the end of the row and, unlike RL-205, flat on its belly. The RL-202, RL-203, and RL-201 were in pieces, but his early-morning tour of the area confirmed that the RL-204 was intact. Barbour even mused to his boss, Wilhelm "Woo" Shaw, about the possibility of a plan like his working.

Signing in that evening at the security gate was no problem, and Barbour immediately deked out of the hangar and slipped into the experimental flight test section. Moving stealthily in the dark along the row of Arrows, he stumbled noisily over the remains of RL-201's wings. Pausing for a few moments to ensure he hadn't been heard, Barbour found a set of tools in a tool crib and prepared a mule. Returning to RL-204 to hitch up the tow bar, he stared into the darkness, trying to make out its shape. Something was wrong. The plane hunched down on its front undercarriage leg, but the nose wheel had been cut off. Shaw! Now Barbour remembered on his morning visit that he had seen his boss take the foreman off to the side. Abandoning the mule, he stormed off in a rage. When the guard at the gatehouse greeted him with the request to sign out, he angrily refused and stalked off into the night. It would be the last time he saw the Arrows.

Today, the Avro CF-105 Arrow is only a memory, although the nose and front landing gear of RL-206, the outer wing panels of RL-203, and an Avro Iroquois engine are displayed in the Canada Aviation Museum. Ironically, the chopped-up nose section of the Avro Jetliner sits nearby. Visitors often marvel at the sleek lines of the Avro Arrow, but are saddened when they notice the jagged end of the cockpit where, years before, wreckers had sawn and chopped it apart.

At the back of the same museum is a Boeing Bomarc missile. The Bomarc proved to be an expensive dud that was removed from service after just a few years, only to be replaced by the McDonnell CF-101 Voodoo. Prime Minister Diefenbaker had reluctantly ordered this American fighter to replace the long-departed Arrow. A prime argument he had invoked in cancelling the Arrow was that the manned interceptor had been "overtaken by events" in the missile age. Recently released Cabinet documents reveal that Diefenbaker recognized the political ramifications of ordering a successor for the Avro Arrow. Only after the chiefs of staff demanded a replacement for the obsolete CF-100 was the Canadian government forced to act. Some military advisors poignantly noted that the Voodoo had been rejected as unsuitable in the initial development of the Avro Arrow.

As of this writing, despite the efforts of a group of historians and concerned citizens in Toronto, the Avro hangars and Administration Building have been demolished. Janusz Zurakowski had once written, "It is impossible to destroy everything ... Governments and torches can destroy an aircraft but they cannot destroy hope and aspiration, and the majesty of the questing spirit. In the hearts of the people, the dream lives on."

Epilogue

They collectively call themselves "Arrowheads." Some grew up with the attributes of the Avro Arrow resonating through family discussions and faded memories, others have only recently discovered the story of the fabled aircraft. All have yearned for a return of this "Golden Age" in Canada's aviation heritage.

Museums across Canada have, of late, devoted their attention to the Avro Arrow legend. Arrow memorabilia exist in various aviation collections in Calgary, Hamilton, Ottawa, and Winnipeg. The West Parry Sound District Museum located at Avro's former Nobel test establishment, created an exhibit in 2000 called the Avro Arrow: A Dream Denied. Based on surviving Arrow and Iroquois components, the display sets out to chronicle historical and personal accounts using original artefacts relating to the Avro Arrow. The exhibit is now on an extended tour across Canada, "playing to packed houses."

Organizations in recent years have been founded to preserve the legacy of the Avro Arrow. The most prominent is the Aerospace Heritage Foundation of Canada (AHFC). Headquartered in Toronto, its members include former Avro employees, as well as numerous enthusiasts. Recently one of the Arrowheads' prized Arrow "treasures" has been located. In 1999, marine mechanic Tom Gartshore set out on a quest using modern technology and one of the original Richardson cruisers constructed by Avro in its waning days to recover a test model launched from the Pt. Petre test range. Bobbing up and down on the choppy Lake Ontario breakers, his side-scan sonar came to life, beeping out the location of one of the nine metal models buried deep in the silt 80 to 102 metres below. The AHFC, in partnership with Arrow Recovery Canada headed by Scott McArthur, has waded into the recovery effort, receiving exclusive ownership of the Arrow models from Crown Assets disposal.

Not far from the original Avro and Orenda factories in Toronto, the Avro Arrow has been reborn. Unlike recent recreations such as the movie model used in the CBC television mini-series, *The Arrow*, the Toronto Aerospace Museum at Downsview Park has embarked on an ambitious multi-year project to faithfully replicate the Arrow. Since 1998, the museum has undertaken the task of preserving the aviation heritage of the Toronto area, which included the Curtiss-Wright, de Havilland, and A.V. Roe Canada companies. At the back of the museum, a Victory Aircraft-built Avro Lancaster bomber is being restored after three decades of display at Ontario Place. It will go on display alongside the recreation of the Avro Arrow to form the showpieces of the museum.

The Avro Arrow replica crew, led by Claude Sherwood, is composed of volunteers, many of whom are ex-Avro

Canada staff. Sherwood's background with the Avro story began in 1956, when he was hired as a draftsman at the age of 18 to work on the CF-105 Arrow. Three years later, along with thousands of other Avro employees, he was out of work, but landed back on his feet with a position at the Ontario Department of Transportation. After a lengthy career with the department, he retired and became one of the leading figures in the formation of the Toronto Aerospace Museum. Dating back from his final days at Avro, Sherwood located technical drawings that he had "squirreled away" and on the basis of these drawings, the Avro Arrow project was created.

The steel-framed replica now has a cockpit and nose section, fuselage, tail, and various outer wing panels completed. One of the project dilemmas was building the Arrow's complex landing gear. Messier-Dowty built and donated new versions of the original undercarriage units. Other industry partners include Associated Tube who donated 3000 metres of stainless-steel tube, Sico who provided paint, and Bombardier Aerospace, who looked after related tools and hardware necessary for the project.

The initial plans that Sherwood and Paul Cabot, the museum director, had formulated involved introducing the recreated Avro Arrow to the public with its first test pilot, Janusz Zurakowski, in the cockpit. Sadly, the famed pilot passed away on February 9, 2004, in his hometown of Barry's Bay, Ontario, after courageously battling leukemia for years. When the Avro Arrow replica eventually takes its place at the museum, Zura will undoubtedly be looking down, perhaps with a sly smile, knowing that the Arrow has finally made it back home.

Bibliography

The Arrow. Directed by Don McBrearty. CBC./Filmworks, 1997, Four-hour mini-series.

Campagna, Palmiro. *Requiem for a Giant: A.V. Roe Canada and the Avro Arrow.* Toronto: Dundern Press, 2003.

Dixon, Joan and Nicholas Kostyan Dixon. *Made for Canada: The Story of Avro's Arrow.* Calgary: A.V. Roe Canada Heritage Museum, 2001.

Dow, James. *The Arrow.* Toronto: James Lorrimer and Co., 1979.

Floyd, James C. *The Avro Canada C102 Jetliner.* Erin, Ontario: Boston Mills Press, 1986.

Gainor, Chris. *Arrows to the Moon: Avro's Engineers and the Space Race.* Burlington, Ontario: Apogee Books, 2001.

Milberry, Larry. *The Avro CF-100.* Toronto: CANAV Books, 1981.

Organ, Richard, Ron Page, Don Watson and Les Wilkinson. *Arrow.* Erin, Ontario: Boston Mills Press, 1980, 1993 (2nd edition).

Page, Betty. *Mynarski's Lanc: The story of two famous Canadian Lancaster Bombers K726 & FM213.* Erin, Ontario: Boston Mills Press, 1989.

Page, Ron D. *CF-100 Canuck: All-weather Fighter.* Erin, Ontario: Boston Mills Press, 1981.

Peden, Murray. *Fall of An Arrow.* Toronto: Stoddart, 1978.

Rossiter, Sean. *The Chosen Ones: Canada's Test Pilots in Action.* Vancouver: Douglas & McIntyre, 2002.

Shaw, E.K. *There Never Was an Arrow.* Brampton, Ontario: Steel Rail, 1981.

Stewart, Greig. *Arrow through the Heart: The Life and Times of Crawford Gordon and the Avro Arrow,* Scarborough, Ontario: McGraw-Hill Ryerson, 1998.

Shutting Down the National Dream. Scarborough, Ontario: McGraw-Hill Ryerson, 1997.

Whitcomb, Randall. *Avro Aircraft and Cold War Aviation.*

St. Catharine's, Ontario: Vanwell Publishing, 2002.

Zuk, Bill. *Avrocar: Canada's Flying Saucer: The Story of Avro Canada's Secret Projects.* Erin, Ontario: Boston Mills Press, 2001.

Janusz Zurakowski: Legend in the Skies. St. Catharines, Ontario: Vanwall Publishing, 2004.

Zuuring, Peter. *The Arrow Scrapbook: Rebuilding a Dream and a Nation.* Ottawa: Arrow Alliance Press, 1999.

Arrow Alliance Press, Kingston, Ontario:
Arrow Countdown. 2001
Arrow First Flight. 2002
Arrow Rollout. 2002
Iroquois Rollout. 2002

For the true "Arrowheads" out there, don't forget to visit the Canada Aviation Museum in Ottawa to see the Arrow and Jetliner cadavers; the Reynold Alberta Aviation Museum in Wetaskawin, Alberta, to see the full-size CBC movie *Arrow*; the Toronto Aerospace Museum to see the Arrow replica; the Western Canada Aviation Museum to see the Avrocar movie model; and Zurakowski Park in Barry's Bay, Ontario, to see a life-size statue of Janusz Zurakowski and a one-quarter scale Avro Arrow.

Acknowledgements

This work would not be possible without the love and support of my family.

Photo Credits

Cover: Canadian Aviation Museum; DND photo: pages 17, 32, 50, 92; Jim Floyd collection: page 41; Herb Nott collection: page 110; Ontario Provincial Archives: page 24; J. Zurakowski collection: page 59.

About the Author

Bill Zuk is an aviation historian and author whose interest in the Avro Arrow dates back to a time when he was an Air Cadet. He is an active member of the Canadian Aviation Historical Society and the Western Canada Aviation Museum. Currently a teacher-librarian in Pembina Trails School Division in Winnipeg, he also works as the training coordinator for the aviation industry in Manitoba. His writing career began in 1997 when he was involved in the Arrow mini-series. He is the author of *Avrocar: Canada's Flying Saucer* and *Janusz Zurakowski: Legend in the Skies.* He also worked on the documentary *Avrocar: Saucer Secrets from the Past,* which was based on his book. He was able to fulfill an improbable dream of actually building a flying saucer, albeit, a movie version. In 2003, he served as the curator of a travelling exhibition, *The Avro Arrow: A Dream is Denied* and directed two film documentaries, *Bearing His Soul* and *Zero Over the Prairies,* for CTV and PBS.

AMAZING STORIES

also available!

UNSUNG HEROES OF THE ROYAL CANADIAN AIR FORCE

Incredible Tales of Courage and Daring During World War II

"That he was a hero is merely incidental to the fact that he died in pain — that he was robbed of life — and that he is lost to his generation. There is glory in living for an ideal as well as in dying for it."
Hector Bolitho, 1946

More than 250,000 courageous men and women were enlisted in the Royal Canadian Air Force during World War II. These Canadians fought valiantly in every major air operation from the Battle of Britain to the bombing of Germany. Thousands lost their lives. Those who survived to tell their stories were forever changed. Here are some of their incredible stories.

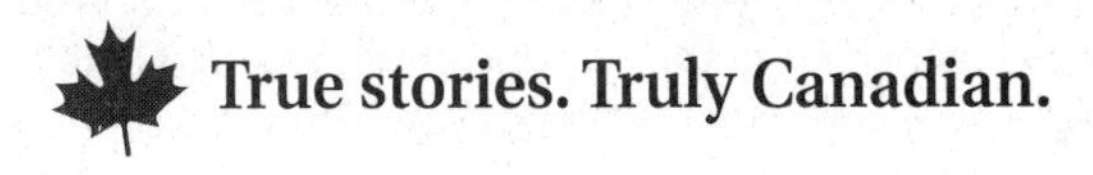

ISBN 1-55153-977-2

OTHER AMAZING STORIES

ISBN	Title	Author
1-55153-943-8	Black Donnellys	Nate Hendley
1-55153-947-0	Canada's Rumrunners	Art Montague
1-55153-966-7	Canadian Spies	Tom Douglas
1-55153-795-8	D-Day	Tom Douglas
1-55153-982-9	Dinosaur Hunters	Lisa Murphy-Lamb
1-55153-970-5	Early Voyageurs	Marie Savage
1-55153-968-3	Edwin Alonzo Boyd	Nate Hendley
1-55153-996-9	Emily Carr	Cat Klerks
1-55153-973-X	Great Canadian Love Stories	Cheryl MacDonald
1-55153-946-2	Great Dog Stories	Roxanne Snopek
1-55153-942-X	The Halifax Explosion	Joyce Glasner
1-55153-958-6	Hudson's Bay Company Adventures	Elle Andra-Warner
1-55153-969-1	Klondike Joe Boyle	Stan Sauerwein
1-55153-980-2	Legendary Show Jumpers	Debbie G-Arsenault
1-55153-979-9	Ma Murray	Stan Sauerwein
1-55153-964-0	Marilyn Bell	Patrick Tivy
1-55153-953-5	Moe Norman	Stan Sauerwein
1-55153-962-4	Niagara Daredevils	Cheryl MacDonald
1-55153-945-4	Pierre Elliott Trudeau	Stan Sauerwein
1-55153-981-0	Rattenbury	Stan Sauerwein
1-55153-991-8	Rebel Women	Linda Kupecek
1-55153-956-X	Robert Service	Elle Andra-Warner
1-55153-952-7	Strange Events	Johanna Bertin
1-55153-954-3	Snowmobile Adventures	Linda Aksomitis
1-55153-950-0	Tom Thomson	Jim Poling Sr.
1-55153-976-4	Trailblazing Sports Heroes	Joan Dixon
1-55153-977-2	Unsung Heroes of the RCAF	Cynthia J. Faryon
1-55153-959-4	A War Bride's Story	Cynthia Faryon
1-55153-948-9	The War of 1812 Against the States	Jennifer Crump

These titles are available wherever you buy books. If you have trouble finding the book you want, call the Altitude order desk at 1-800-957-6888, e-mail your request to: orderdesk@altitudepublishing.com or visit our Web site at www.amazingstories.ca

New AMAZING STORIES titles are published every month.